The Children's Book of Birds

by Olive Thorne Miller

Copyright © 4/7/2016
Jefferson Publication

ISBN-13: 978-1530948987

Printed in the United States of America

Table of Contents

I

WHAT YOU WANT TO KNOW

Birds seem to be the happiest creatures on earth, yet they have none of what we call the comforts of life.

They have no houses to live in, no beds to sleep on, no breakfast and dinner provided for them.

This book is to tell something about them; where they live and what they eat, where they sleep, how they get their beautiful dress, and many other things. But no one can tell all about their lives and habits, for no one knows all their ways.

Men who study dead birds can tell how they are made, how their bones are put together, and how many feathers there are in the wings and tail. Of course it is well to know these things. But to see how birds live is much more interesting than to look at dead ones.

It is pleasant to see how mother birds build their nests, and how they take care of their nestlings. It is charming to see the young ones when they begin to fly, and to know how they are taught to find their food, and to keep out of danger, and to sing, and everything young birds need to know.

Then when they are grown up, it is interesting to find out where they go in winter, and why they do not stay with us all the year round.

One who goes into the field to watch and study their ways will be surprised to find how much like people they act. And after studying living birds, he will never want to kill them. It will seem to him almost like murder.

II

WHEN THEY COME IN THE SPRING

In the long, cold winter of the New England and Middle States, not many birds are usually seen. In the cities there is always the English sparrow, and in the country, now and then a chickadee, or a woodpecker, or a small flock of goldfinches.

But very early in the spring, long before grass is green, even while snow is on the ground, the birds begin to come.

Some morning a robin will appear, standing up very straight on a fence or tree, showing his bright red breast and black cap, flirting his tail, and looking as if he were glad to be back in his old home.

5

Then perhaps the same day will come the hoarse chack of a blackbird, and two or three will fly over and alight in a big bare tree, looking, it may be, for a good place to build a bird city.

Soon will be heard the sweet little song of the song sparrow or the bluebird, and then we shall know that summer is coming, for these are the first birds of spring.

Day after day, as the snow melts away and the sunshine grows hotter, more birds will come. One day a catbird or two, another day an oriole in black and gold, and another day a pert little wren. So it will go on, till by the time June comes in, all our birds will be back with us, very busy, hopping around in our bushes and trees, making their nests all about, and singing the whole day long.

Almost the first thing every bird thinks of, when he comes to us, is making the nest. For summer is the only time in his life that a bird has a home.

He does not need a house to live in. He cares nothing for a roof to cover him, because when the sun is hot, he has the broad green leaves on the trees to shade him. And when it rains his neat feather coat is like a waterproof that lets the drops run off, leaving him warm and dry under it.

He does not need a dining-room, because he eats wherever he finds his food, and he wants no kitchen, because he prefers his food raw.

He has no use for a bedroom, because he can sleep on any twig; the whole world is his bedroom.

He cares nothing for closets and bureaus, because he has only one suit of clothes at a time, and he washes and dries that without taking it off.

He wants no fire to keep him warm, for when it is too cold he spreads his wings and flies to a warmer place. A bird has really no need of a house,—excepting when he is a baby, before his eyes are open, or his feathers have come, or his wings have grown. While he is blind, naked, and hungry, he must have a warm, snug cradle.

So when the bird fathers and mothers come in the spring the first thing they do is to find good places and build nice cradles, for they are very fond of their little ones. They spend the spring and summer in working for them, keeping them warm, feeding them till they are grown up, and then teaching them to fly and to take care of themselves, so that when summer is gone they will be ready to go with the other birds to their winter home.

THE NESTLING

III

THE BIRD'S HOME

Each bird mother has her own way of making the nest, but there is one thing almost all of them try to do, and that is to hide it.

They cannot put their little homes out in plain sight, as we do our houses, because so many creatures want to rob them. Squirrels and snakes and rats, and some big birds, and cats and many others, like to eat eggs and young birds.

So most birds try, first of all, to find good hiding-places. Some tiny warblers go to the tops of the tallest trees, and hide the nest among the leaves. Orioles hang the swinging cradle at the end of a branch, where cats and snakes and naughty boys cannot come. Song sparrows tuck the little home in a tuft of weeds, on the ground, and bobolinks hide it in the deep grass.

After a safe place is found, they have to get something to build of. They hunt all about and gather small twigs, or grass stems, or fine rootlets, and pull narrow strips of bark off the grapevines and the birch-trees, or they pick up strings and horsehairs, and many other things. Robins and swallows use mud.

BALTIMORE ORIOLE AND NEST

As they go on building, the mother bird gets inside and turns around and around to make it fit her form, and be smooth and comfortable for her to sit in.

When a nest is made, it must be lined. Then some birds go to the chicken yard, and pick up feathers, and others find horsehairs. Some of them pull off the soft down that grows on plants, or get bits of wool from the sheep pasture, or old leaves from the woods, and make it soft and warm inside.

Some bird homes are only platforms, where it seems as if the eggs must roll off, and others are deep burrows, or holes in the ground, where no one can get in. Some are dainty baskets hung between two twigs, and others are tiny cups of felt with lichens outside.

Each species of bird builds in its own way. There are as many different ways to make nests as there are kinds of birds to make them.

Then after all the trouble birds have taken to build a nest, they seldom use it a second time. If a pair have two broods in a season, they almost always build a new one for each family.

A few birds, such as eagles, owls, and sometimes orioles, and others, repair the home and use it again, and woodpeckers sometimes nest in the old holes. But generally, after the young birds have flown, we may be sure the nest will not be wanted again.

When the nest is finished, the eggs are laid in it, one by one. We all know how pretty birds' eggs are. Some are snowy white, some are delicate pink, and some blue. Many have tiny dots and specks on them, and a few are covered with queer-looking streaks and lines. But pretty as they are, I think no one would be so cruel as to take them away from the poor little mother, if he remembered that her young ones are inside them, and that she loves them as his own mother loves him.

I have heard people say that birds do not care for their eggs. Let me tell you what a little chickadee mother did when a man tried to steal the eggs out of her nest.

7

The nest was in a hole in an old stump, and the man could not get his hand in, so he had to take them out one at a time with a little scoop.

At first the mother flew at him and tried to drive him away. Then chickadees and other birds who lived near came to help her. All flew about his face with cries, so that he had to use one hand to keep them away from his eyes. But still he went on taking out the eggs.

At last the little mother was so wild with grief that she dashed into the hole and sat there in the doorway, right before his face. He could not get another egg without hurting her, and he was ashamed to do that.

This was as brave in the tiny creature as it would be for a human mother to throw herself before a fierce, hungry tiger. Do you think she did not care for her eggs?

IV

THE BABY BIRD

A baby bird, as you know, always comes out of an egg. And beautiful as these eggs are, they are most interesting when you think that each one holds a tiny bird.

Eggs are not all alike, of course. One the size of a bean is large enough to hold a hummingbird baby, till it is old enough to come out. But the young ostrich needs a shell nearly as big as your head. So there are all sizes of eggs to fit the different sizes of birds.

If you should break a fresh egg you would not see a bird, for it would not be formed at that time. After the egg is laid in its soft bed, it has to be kept warm for many days, and that is why the mother bird sits on her nest so quietly. She is keeping the eggs warm, so that the little ones will form and grow, till they are as big as the shells can hold.

While the mother is sitting her mate does all he can to help, though each species has its own way. The blue jay brings food to his mate, so that she need not leave the nest at all, and many others do so. But the kingbird father simply watches the nest to protect it while the mother goes for food. A redstart gets into the nest himself, to keep the eggs warm while his mate is gone, and a goldfinch coaxes his mate to go off with him for a lunch, leaving nest and eggs to take care of themselves.

REDSTARTS (FEMALE ON NEST)

Another thing the father birds do is to sing. This is the time when we hear so much bird song. The singers have little to do but to wait, and so they please themselves, and their mates, and us too, by singing a great deal.

When the little birds begin to be cramped, and find their cradle too tight, they peck at the shell with a sort of tooth that grows on the end of the beak, and is called the "egg tooth." This soon breaks the shell, and they come out. Then the mother or father carefully picks up the pieces of shell, carries them off, and throws them away, leaving only the little ones in the nest. Perhaps you have found these broken shells on the ground sometimes, and could not guess how they came there. When the birdlings break out of their prison they do not all look the same. Ducks and geese and chickens and quails, and other birds who live on the ground, as well as hawks and owls, are dressed in pretty suits of down. They have their eyes open, and the ground birds are ready to run about at once.

A man who studied birds, once saw a young duck get its first suit of down. He picked up the egg just as the little bird inside was trying to get out. In a few minutes the shell fell apart, and out stepped the duckling on his hand. It seemed to be covered with coarse black hairs, which in a moment began to burst open, one by one, and out of each came a soft fluff of down. So in a few minutes, while the man stood there and held him, the little duck was all covered with his pretty dress.

But most birds hatched in nests in trees and bushes, like robins and bluebirds, are very different. When they come out of their shells they are naked, have their eyes shut, and look as if they were nearly all mouth. A young hummingbird looks about as big as a honey bee, and a robin baby not much bigger than the eggshell he came out of.

They lie flat down in the nest, seeming to be asleep most of the time. All they want is to be warm and to be fed.

To keep them warm, the mother sits on them a great part of the time, and for the first few days of their lives, the father often brings most of the food. Sometimes he gives it to the mother, and she feeds the little ones. But sometimes she gets off the nest, and flies away to rest, and get something to eat for herself, while he feeds the nestlings.

9

There is one bird father who—it is thought—never comes to the nest, either to watch the eggs or to help feed the nestlings. That is our hummingbird, the ruby throat.

We do not know the reason for this, and it is not fair to say hard things about him until we do. It may be that he thinks his shining ruby would show the hiding-place of the nest, or it may be that the little mother is not willing to have any help. I think this last is the real reason, for she has a great deal of spirit, and always drives away others from her feeding-places.

Young birds grow very fast, and soon feathers begin to come out all over them. They are not very pretty at this time.

V

HOW HE IS FED

Soon after the young bird comes out of the egg, he begins to be hungry. All day long, whenever the father or mother comes near, he opens his great mouth as wide as he can, to have it filled, and the moment he gets his voice he cries for food.

Then the old birds have to work hard. Three or four hungry nestlings can keep both father and mother busy from morning till night, hunting for caterpillars and beetles and grubs and other things to feed them. It seems as if the little fellows never could get enough to eat. Each swallow baby wants seven or eight hundred small flies every day, and a baby robin needs more earthworms in a day than you can hold in your hand at once.

At this time you will see robins hunting over the lawn, and carrying great beakfuls of worms up to the nest. Bluebirds you will find looking in the grass, and sparrows hopping about on the ground, all seeking soft worms and grubs and insects for the nestlings; and they are so busy they do not get much time for singing.

RUBY-

THROATED HUMMINGBIRD

At this time the orioles go all over the orchard trees looking for tiny worms, and little warblers seek them under every leaf.

Woodpeckers find the insects hidden behind the bark of trees, by cutting holes through it. Chickadees and nuthatches pick the tiniest insect eggs out of the crevices, and flickers hunt everywhere for ants.

As soon as one of the old birds has his mouth full, he flies to the nest to feed the young.

But not all birds feed in the same way. A robin just drops a big earthworm, or a part of one, into the gaping baby mouth. Many other birds do so also. Sometimes, when an insect is too big or too hard, they beat it till it is soft, or break it up, before giving it to a little one.

But hummingbird mothers and flicker mothers have a different way. When they collect the food they swallow it, as if they wanted it for themselves. Then they go to the nest, and jerk it up again in mouthfuls, and feed the nestlings. This is called feeding by "regurgitation," or "throwing up."

The way they give the food is very curious. They push their long beaks into the nestling's throat, and poke the food far down; so the young one does not even have the trouble of swallowing.

This looks as if it must hurt, but the nestling seems to like it, and is always ready for more. The pigeon mother lets the young one poke his beak down her throat, and get the food for himself.

If the food is hard, like corn, birds who feed in this way let it stay in the crop till it is soft and better fitted for tender throats, before they give it out.

It is comical to see a nest full of little birds when the father or mother comes with food. All stretch up and open their big mouths as wide as they can, and if they are old enough, they cry as if they were starving.

Some birds bring food enough for all in the nest, every time they come. A cedar-bird, feeding wild cherries, brought five of them every time, one for each of the five nestlings. One cherry was held in his mouth, but the other four were down his throat, and had to be jerked up one by one.

Other birds bring only one mouthful at a time, and when there are five or six in the nest, they have to make as many journeys before all are fed.

Some persons who have studied birds think that each nestling is fed in its turn; but they look so much alike, and are so close together, that it is hard to tell, and I am not sure that it is so.

I will tell you a story I have heard about feeding little birds. A child picked up a young goldfinch who had fallen out of the nest. He took him home and put him into the canary's cage, which was hanging on the front porch.

Soon the family heard a great noise among the birds, and went out to see what was the matter. The baby goldfinch had hopped on to a perch in the cage, and seemed to be afraid to come down, though the old birds had brought food for him, and were calling him to take it.

The canary looked on a while, and then all at once he flew to the wires and took the food from the birds outside; then he went back to the perch beside the little one and gave it to him. This he did many times.

The next day another young goldfinch was picked up and put in the cage, and the canary took food from the parents and fed both.

After a few days the old birds came with a third little one, and as all were now old enough to fly, the cage door was opened, and they all flew away.

VI

HIS FIRST SUIT

Some birds that live on the ground—as I told you—have dresses of down to begin with. These little fellows have no warm nest to stay in, but run around almost as soon as they come out of the egg. Young ducks and geese wear this baby suit for weeks, before they begin to put on their feather coats.

Young birds that spend most of their time in the water, like grebes, and others that live in a cold country, have the down very thick and fine, like heavy underclothes, to keep them dry and warm.

Birds whose home is underground, like the kingfisher, or in the trunk of a tree, like the woodpecker, have hardly any down at all. They need no baby clothes in their warm cradles.

Robins and most other song birds have only a little down on them, and very soon the feathers begin to grow.

When the tiny quills push themselves up, they look like little white pins sticking out all over. Each bit of down grows out of a little raised place on the skin that looks like a pimple, and the feather comes out of the same.

YOUNG WOOD THRUSH

As the feather grows, the bit of down clings to it till it is broken off. Sometimes it holds on till the feather is well out. We can often see down sticking to a young bird's feathers.

The little feathers grow very fast, and before he is ready to fly a young bird is well covered. Birds hatched with their eyes open, and already dressed, who have to run and fly very soon, get their wing feathers early; but birds who live many days in the nest, like robins and bluebirds, do not get theirs till they are nearly grown.

The tail feathers are the last to come to full length, and you will notice that most birds just out of the nest have very dumpy tails.

A bird's first suit of feathers is called his nestling plumage. In some families it is just like the dress of the grown-up birds, but in others it is not at all like that. It is usually worn only a few weeks, for the young one outgrows it, and needs a new and bigger one before winter.

When a bird is fully dressed, his body is entirely covered, and it looks as if the feathers grew close to each other all over him. But it is not so. The feathers grow in patterns, called "feather tracts," with spaces of bare skin between them. These bare places do not show, because the feathers lap over each other and cover them.

The pattern of the feather tracts is not the same in all birds. A few birds of the Ostrich family have feathers all over the body.

There is another curious thing about the nestling plumage. You would expect a young bird to look like his father or mother; and some of them do. Many nestlings are dressed exactly like their mothers; and not until they are a year old do the young males get a coat like their father's. Some of them, indeed, do not have their grown-up suits for two or three years.

Then, again, many young birds have dresses different from both parents. Young robins have speckled breasts, and spots on the shoulders, which the old birds have not.

When the father and mother are dressed alike, as the song sparrows are, the young birds generally differ from both of them. When the father and mother are different, like orioles or bluebirds, the young are usually like the mother the first season. In some cases the father, mother, and young are almost exactly alike.

Birds who live on the ground need dresses of dull colors, or they would not be very safe. The ostrich mother, who makes her nest in plain sight on the sand, is dressed in grayish brown. When she sits on the eggs, she lays her long neck flat on the ground before her; then she looks like one of the ant-hills that are common on the plains of Africa, where she lives.

The South American ostrich, or rhea, fluffs out her feathers and looks like a heap of dry grass. The male ostrich is dressed in showy black and white, and he stays away all day, but takes care of the nest at night, when his striking colors cannot be seen.

VII

HOW HE CHANGES HIS CLOTHES

It takes a bird weeks to put on a new suit of clothes. He has nothing but his feathers to protect him from cold and wet, and as feathers cannot grow out in a minute, he would be left naked, and suffer, if he lost them all at once. So he changes his dress one or two feathers at a time.

Some day a feather will drop from each wing. If you could look, you would see that new ones had started out in the same place, and pushed the old ones off. When the new ones are pretty well grown another pair will fall out.

If all dropped out at once, besides suffering with cold he would not be able to fly, and he could not get his living, and anybody could catch him. But losing only one from each side at a time, he always has enough to fly with.

It is the same way with his tail feathers. He loses them in pairs, one from each side at the same time.

AMERICAN GOLDFINCH

The soft feathers that cover his body drop out one by one. Thus all the time he is putting on a new suit he still wears part of the old one. In this way he is never left without clothes for a moment.

Most birds put on their new suits just after the young ones are grown up, and before they all start for the South to spend the winter,—that is, with many of our common birds, in August. At that time they are rather shy, and stop singing. If you did not see one now and then, you might think they were all gone.

Sometimes the new fall suit is not at all like the old one. There is the goldfinch, all summer in bright yellow. When he comes out in his new suit in August, it is dull-colored, much like the one his mate wears all the year, and in winter, when goldfinches fly around in little flocks, they look nearly all alike.

In the spring, the male goldfinch comes out again in yellow. He has two suits a year,—a bright yellow one in the spring, and a dull olive-green for the winter. But his new spring dress is not a full suit. The yellow of the body is all fresh, but the black wings are the same the year round.

Some birds have two, different colored dresses in a year; one they get without changing a feather. Suppose they have feathers of black, with gray on the outside edges. All winter the gray shows and the birds seem to have gray coats. But in spring the gray edges wear or fall off, and the black shows, and then they look as if they had come out in new black suits. It is as if you should take off a gray overcoat and show a black coat under it.

There is another interesting thing about birds' dress. Some of them look like their mates, the father and mother birds so nearly alike that it is hard, sometimes impossible, to tell them apart. But when that is the case, you will notice that the color is not very gay. If the father wears a bright-colored suit, the mother does not look like him.

For this reason the little mother is not too easily seen when she is on her nest. If the goldfinch mother were as bright as her mate, everybody who came near would see her on the nest, and some animal might take her, and leave the young birds to starve to death. That is probably why mother birds dress in such dull colors.

When birds live on the ground, or very near it, in most cases both of the pair wear the dull colors, so they will not easily be seen. Wrens and sparrows and many others are so. But birds who make their nests in holes, or under ground, are often as bright as their mates, because they cannot be seen while sitting, and do not need to wear dull colors.

A curious thing about a bird's color is that the same species, or kind of bird, is darker in one place than another. Where there is much dampness or wet weather, the colors are darker. For instance, a bob-white who lives in Florida, or one who lives in Oregon, will be much darker than his cousin living in New England.

VIII

HIS FIRST FLIGHT

When young birds are in the nest they are not very pretty. But when they are nearly feathered, and sit up on the edge, exercising their wings, and getting ready to fly, they are lovely to look at. Their feathers are more fluffy and fresh than those of the old birds.

At that time they have not learned to be afraid of us, and if we do not frighten them by roughness, loud talking, or quick movements, we can often get near enough to see them well. They will sit up and look at us without fear.

Then some day, all at once, a young bird will begin to flap his wings, and off he will go, fluttering very hard, beating his wings, and trying to reach the next tree.

Sometimes he will reach it, and perch on a twig, and sit quite still a long time, tired with his first flight. Then the parents will come and feed him, and after a while he will fly again. This time he will go farther.

So he will go on, till in a few days he can fly very well, and follow his parents about, and begin to learn where to get food.

Sometimes when a young bird leaves the nest he does not reach the tree he starts for, but falls to the ground. Then there is trouble among the birds. He is in danger of being picked up by a cat or a boy, or of getting tangled in the grass or weeds.

The poor parents are half wild with fear. They coax him to try again, and they follow him about in the grass, in great distress. I have many times picked up a little bird, and set him on a branch of a tree, or stood guard over him, driving away cats and keeping off people, till he reached a place where he would be safe.

When young birds are out, but cannot yet fly very well, there is much anxiety about them. Then, if any one comes around to disturb them, what can the poor little mother do? Sometimes she makes her young ones hide. Some of the birds who live on the ground will give a certain cry, when in a second every little one will crouch on the ground, or creep under a leaf, and be perfectly still. And their dark colors look so like the earth one can hardly see them.

Then the mother tries to make one look at her by queer antics. She pretends to be hurt, and tumbles about as if she could not fly. If it is a man or an animal who has frightened her, he will usually think he can easily catch her; so he will forget about the young ones, and follow her as she goes fluttering over the ground. She will go on playing that she is hurt, and moving away, till she leads him far from her brood. Then she will start up and fly away, and he cannot find his way back to where the little ones are still crouching.

Sometimes when a mother is frightened, she will snatch up her young one between her feet, and fly away with it. Sometimes a mother will fight, actually fly into the face of the one she fears. Often, too, other birds come to her aid; birds of many kinds,—catbirds, robins, thrashers, and others,—all come to help her drive away the enemy, for birds are almost always ready to help each other.

I once found a young blue jay who had come to the ground while trying his first flight. I thought I would pick him up and put him on a branch. But the old birds did not know what I meant to do, and perhaps they were afraid I would carry him off.

They flew at me with loud cries to drive me away, and I thought it best to go, for I did not want to make them any more unhappy than they were already.

I did not go far, because I wanted to see that no one caught the little one. He hopped about in the grass a long time, while his parents flew around him in great distress. Many times he tried to fly, but he could not rise more than two feet from the ground.

At last he seemed to make up his mind to climb a tree, for when he came to one with a rough bark he began to go up. He would fly up a few inches, then hold on with his claws to rest. And so, half flying and half climbing, he went on till he reached the lowest limb. On that he perched and was quiet, glad to rest after his hard work. The old birds were happy, too, and brought food to him, and so I left them.

IX

HIS EDUCATION

The young bird has to be educated, or trained for his life, just as we do, though not exactly in the same way.

He does not have to know arithmetic and history; and what he needs of geography is only the road to the South, where he spends his winters.

I suppose the first thing he learns is to fly. You have heard, perhaps, that the old birds drive their young out of the nest. But do not believe any such thing, for it is not true. I have seen many little birds leave the nest, and almost every one flew when the parents were away after food.

The parents sometimes try to coax a nestling who is afraid to try his wings, like an oriole I knew of. All the young orioles had flown except this one, and he seemed to be too timid to try. He stood on the edge of the nest, and called and cried, but did not use his wings.

The father came to see him now and then, and at last he made him fly in this way. He caught a fine, large moth, and brought it to the nest in his beak. The young bird was very hungry, and when he saw the food, he opened his mouth and fluttered his wings, so eager to get it he could hardly wait.

But the parent did not feed him. He let him see the moth, and then, with a loud call, he flew to the next tree. When the little oriole saw the food going away, he forgot he was afraid, and with a cry of horror he sprang after it; and so, before he knew it, he had flown.

After the young bird can fly, he needs to be taught to get his own living, or to find his own food, and also where to sleep. Then he must learn what to be afraid of, and how to protect himself from his enemies.

He needs to know the different calls and cries of his family, and what they all mean. He has to learn to fly in a flock with other birds, and he must learn to sing. No doubt there are many more lessons for him that we do not know about.

If you watch little birds just out of the nest, you may see them being taught the most useful and important lesson, how to find their food.

The robin mother takes her little one to the ground, and shows him where the worms live and how to get them. The owl mother finds a mouse creeping about in the grass, and teaches the owlets how to pounce upon it, by doing it herself before them.

The old swallow takes her youngsters into the air, and shows them how to catch little flies on the wing; while mother phœbe teaches hers to sit still and watch till a fly comes near, and then fly out and catch it.

If you watch long enough, after a while you may see the old bird, who is training a young one, fly away. She may leave the young one alone on a tree or the ground, and be gone a long time.

Before many minutes the little one will get hungry, and begin to call for food. But by and by, if nobody comes to feed him, he will think to look around for something to eat. Thus he will get his lesson in helping himself.

Once I saw a woodpecker father bring his little one to a fence, close by some raspberry bushes that were full of berries. He fed him two or three berries, to teach him what they were and where they grew, and then quietly slipped away.

When the young bird began to feel hungry he cried out; but nobody came. Then he looked over at the raspberries, and reached out and tried to get hold of one. After trying three or four times, and nearly pitching off his perch, he did reach one. Then how proud he was!

The father stayed away an hour or more, and before he came back that young woodpecker had learned to help himself very well; though the minute his father came, he began to flutter his wings and beg to be fed, as if he were half starved.

A lady, who fed the wild birds on her window sill for many years, and watched their ways, says she often saw the old birds teaching their little ones. They showed them where the food was to be found, and, she says, regularly taught them the art of eating.

Then she saw them taught to be afraid of people, not to come too near her. And once she saw an old bird showing a young one how to gather twigs for nest-building. The young one looked on a while, and then tried hard to do it himself, but could not get off a single twig.

Best of all, the same lady heard an old robin giving a music lesson. The teacher would sing a few notes and then stop, while the pupil tried to copy them. He had a weak, babyish sort of voice, and did not succeed very well at first.

I have heard several birds at their music lessons.

X

SOME OF HIS LESSONS

It is very easy to catch the birds teaching their little ones to exercise their wings and to fly together. You will see the young birds sitting quietly on fences or trees, when all at once the parents begin to fly around, with strange loud calls. In a minute every youngster will fly out and join them. Around and around they all go, hard as they can, till their little wings are tired, and then they come down and alight again.

Once I saw a young bird who did not go when his parents called. All the others flew around many times, and I suppose that young one thought he would not be noticed.

But mothers' eyes are sharp, and his mother saw him. So when she came back, she flew right at her naughty son, and knocked him off his perch. The next time she called, he flew with the rest. This was a crow mother.

I have seen a bluebird just out of the nest, taught to follow his father in this way. He stood on a small tree, crying for something to eat, when his father came in sight with a beakful of food. He did not feed him, but flew past him, so close that he almost touched him, and alighted on the next tree, a little beyond him.

BLUEBIRD

The little bluebird saw the food, and at once flew after it, perched beside his father, and was fed. Then the old bird left him, and in a few minutes he felt hungry, and began to call again.

I kept close watch, and soon the father came and did the same thing over. He flew past the young one with an insect in plain sight in his beak, and perched on another tree still farther along in the way he wanted the little one to go.

The hungry baby followed, and was fed as before. In this way he was led to a big tree the other side of the yard, where the rest of the family were, and where they all spent the night.

An old robin wanted to teach her young one to bathe. She brought him to a dish of water kept for their use by some people who were fond of birds. The little one stood on the edge and watched his mother go in, and splash and scatter the water. He fluttered his wings, and was eager to try it for himself, but seemed afraid to plunge in.

At last the mother flew away and left him standing there, and in a moment came back with a worm in her mouth. The young robin was hungry, as young birds always are, and when he saw the worm, he began to flutter his wings, and cry for it.

But the mother jumped into the middle of the water dish, and stood there, holding the worm in his sight. The youngster wanted the worm so much that he seemed to forget his fear of the water, and hopped right in beside her. She fed him, and then began to splash about, and he liked it so well that he stayed and took a good bath.

Birds, as these stories show, teach their little ones by coaxing, and not by driving them.

An Englishman, Mr. Lloyd Morgan, once had some ducks and chickens hatched away from their mother, to see how much their parents had to teach them.

17

He found that these little orphans had to be taught to pick up their food, and to know what is good to eat. He had to show the young ducks how to dive, and teach all of them that water is good to drink.

To see if chickens had to be taught the hen language, he put them out by their mother when they were a few days old.

The hen was going about with her brood, all brothers and sisters of Mr. Morgan's chicks, and she was quite ready to adopt the new ones. She clucked and called to them with all her might, but they did not come. They acted as if they did not hear her. When the others ran and crept under her wings to be brooded, the strangers looked on, but did not think of going too.

They did not understand the calls or the ways of their own mother. They had not been taught.

A careful watcher will see the birds teach these things, and many others as interesting. But no one will see anything unless he is quiet, and does not frighten them.

THE BIRD GROWN UP

XI

THE BIRD'S LANGUAGE

When the bird is grown up, there are many other interesting things to know about him,—one is, whether he can talk.

It is plain to those who have studied the ways of birds, that they are able to tell things to each other, and many writers have said plainly that birds have a language.

If you notice birds in cages, you will find that when two or more of a kind are in the same room, you will hear little chirps and twitters and other notes, not at all like their song. But if one is alone in a room, he hardly makes a sound except when singing.

Then see a robin out of doors. He is less afraid of us than most birds, and easiest to watch. If something comes up on him suddenly, he gives a sharp note of surprise. If a cat appears, he has another cry which every one can understand, a word of warning to all. If everything is quiet and his mate is near, he will greet her with some low, sweet notes.

When a partridge mother sees danger, she gives one call, which all her brood know, and at once run and hide. When the hen speaks to her chicks, they know well whether it means to come to her, or to run away.

Of course birds do not use our words. When it is said that the quail says "Bob White," it is meant that his call sounds like those words. To some the notes sound like "more wet." One may call it almost anything, like "all right" or "too hot."

You will read in books about birds, that a certain warbler says "Witches here," or that the white-throated sparrow says "Old Sam Peabody," and other birds say still different things. The writer means that the words remind one of the bird's notes, and so it is useful to know them, because it helps you to know the bird when you hear him.

I have many times seen birds act as if they were talking to each other. You can often see the city sparrows do so.

There is nothing in a bird's ways that we like so well as his singing. And in all the many species of birds in the world, no two sing exactly alike, so far as I can find out. You may always know a bird by his song. A robin does not sing like a thrush or a catbird. And what is more, not one of the sounds he utters is like those made by any other bird. If you know him well, whatever noise he makes, you will know at once that it is a robin.

But there is something still more curious about it. No robin sings exactly like another robin. When you come to know one bird well, you can tell his song from any other bird's. Of course, all robins sing enough alike for one to know that it is a robin song, but if you listen closely, you will see that it is really different from all others.

Persons who have kept birds in cages have noticed the same thing.

There is still another point to know. One bird does not always sing the same song. I have heard a song sparrow sing five or six different songs, standing all the time in plain sight on a fence. In the same way I have known a meadowlark to make six changes in his few notes.

Besides their own natural songs, many birds like to copy the notes of others. Our mockingbird is very fond of learning new things, and he does not always choose songs either.

He will imitate the noise of filing a saw, or the pop of a cork, as readily as the sweetest song. I have heard one sing the canary's song better than the canary himself.

INDIGO-BIRD

Other birds can do the same. A common English sparrow picked up in the streets of a big city, hurt, and not able to fly, was put into a room with a canary.

No doubt the wild bird found his life in a cage rather dull, after having been used to the streets, and he soon began to amuse himself trying to do as the canary did, to sing. In a few weeks he learned the whole song, and he could sing it even better than his roommate, for his voice was full and rich, and not so shrill as the canary's.

Most people think that birds sing all summer. They think so because they have not taken notice. We who are very fond of bird song know it is not so.

Singing begins when the birds first come in the spring. It goes on while the nest is being built, and the mother bird is sitting. The father has little to do at that time, and so he sings. And besides, he seems to be so happy that he cannot help it.

But when little ones begin to call for food, he has to be very busy, and does not have so much time for music. Some birds stop singing as soon as they go to feeding.

But not all do so. Many go on singing till they begin to change their clothes, or to moult, as it is called. This happens in August or September, and when it begins, a bird seems to lose his voice.

One of the first to stop singing is the bobolink. He is rarely heard after June is past. The veery is another whose singing days are over early. You may hear his call in the woods, if you know it, but not a song will you hear after the middle of July.

By the time August comes in, almost every bird is silent, except for his calls or "talk." The birds to be heard then are the red-eyed vireo, who seems never to tire, and now and then the indigo-bird, or the wood pewee, and best of all, the dear little song sparrow, who keeps up his cheery songs till the very last.

19

Then you will know that all the birds are busy putting on their new suits for their long journey.

XII

WHAT HE EATS

What the bird eats and where he gets his food are useful things for us to know. It has only lately been found out that birds are the most valuable of helpers to us.

What we cannot eat ourselves, they are happy to live on, and things that make us a great deal of trouble are their daily food.

Some of the things they are fond of are little animals, like mice and ground squirrels, that eat our crops. Others are insects which spoil our fruit and eat up our vegetables, cankerworms and cutworms, and a hundred more.

Besides these, many birds eat the seeds of certain weeds that farmers have to fight all the time.

One reason this helps us so greatly is that birds eat much more for their size than we do. A boy of six or eight years could not possibly eat a whole sheep in one day, but a young bird can easily eat more than his own weight every day.

They want more than three meals too. They need to eat very often. One catbird will take thirty grasshoppers for his breakfast, and in a few hours he will want thirty more. So he destroys a great many in a day.

Birds begin eating long before we are out of bed, and keep it up till night comes again, or as long as they can see.

You must not think the birds are greedy, as a person would be if he ate every few minutes all day. They are made to do so. It is their business to destroy insects, small animals, and weeds that trouble us so much, and the more they eat the better for us.

Let us see where they go for food. Each bird has his own place to work.

The catbird watches the fruit-trees, and all day long eats insects that are spoiling our fruit or killing the trees. When the cherries are ripe, we should not forget that he has saved the fruit from insects, and has well earned a share for himself.

If you spent days and weeks picking off insects, would you not think you had earned part of the fruit? "For every cherry he eats" (says a man who has watched him), "he has eaten at least one thousand insects."

The robin eats great numbers of cankerworms, which destroy our apples, and cutworms, which kill the corn.

The bluebird sits on the fence keeping sharp watch, and every few minutes flies down and picks up a grasshopper or a cricket, or some such grass-eating insect.

Woodpeckers hunt over the trunks and limbs of trees. They tap on the bark and listen, and if they hear a grub stir inside, they cut a hole in the bark and drag it out. The downy is fond of insects that infest our apple-trees, and he makes many holes in the trunks. But it does not hurt the trees. It is good for them, for it takes away the creatures that were eating them.

Orioles go over the fruit-trees, and pick out tiny insects under the leaves, and when they find great nests on the branches, they tear them open and kill the caterpillars that made them.

Little warblers, such as the pretty summer yellow-bird, help to keep our trees clear, doing most of their work in the tops, where we can hardly see them.

Swallows fly about in the air, catching mosquitoes and tiny flies that trouble us.

Very useful to us are the birds who feed upon dead animals, such as the turkey buzzards, who may be seen any day in our Southern States, soaring about high in the air, looking for their food.

What they eat is so very unpleasant to us that we are apt to despise the birds. But we should cherish and feel grateful to them instead. For they are doing us the greatest kindness. In many of the hot countries people could not live, if these most useful birds were killed.

Some persons think buzzards find their food by seeing it, and others are just as sure that they smell it. Perhaps they use both senses.

XIII

MORE ABOUT HIS FOOD

Some of the big birds work all the time for us. When you see a hawk sitting very still on a dead limb, what do you suppose he is doing?

A good deal of the time he is looking on the ground for a mouse, or a ground squirrel, or a rat, or some creature that he likes to eat.

When he sees one of them move in the grass, he flies down and pounces upon it. Thus he helps the farmer greatly, for all of these little animals destroy crops.

When it grows dark, hawks stop work and go to sleep. Then the owls, who can see better in the dusk, come out of the holes where they have been half sleeping all day. They hunt the same little creatures, most of all rats and mice, which like best to run about in the night.

Perhaps you have heard that hawks and owls carry off chickens. Many people who keep chickens shoot every hawk and owl they see. But if they knew more about them they would not do so. Only two of the common hawks and one owl disturb chickens. All the others kill thousands of the little animals that give the farmers so much trouble.

Owls have a curious way of eating mice. They swallow them whole, and after a while they throw up a queer-looking little ball made of the bones and fur of the mouse.

You may some time have seen a long-legged heron walking about on the seashore or in the salt marsh. Now and then he would thrust his long, sharp bill into something, and lift up his head and swallow. Or you have noticed a little sandpiper running along on the beach or the bank of a river.

The heron was probably eating frogs or fish, and the sandpiper some of the small sea creatures thrown up by the waves. If these were not taken away they would be very bad for us, and perhaps make us sick.

Not less useful to us than these birds are the whole family of finches. The goldfinch in bright yellow coat, the purple finch in red, and the sparrows in plain brown. All of these are fond of seeds as well as insects, and most of all they like the seeds of some weeds that are hard to get rid of.

The goldfinch is called the thistle-bird, because he likes best the seeds of thistles, though he eats the beggar's-ticks too.

The chipping sparrow, the little red-headed bird who comes about our doors, eats the seeds of fox-tail and crab grasses, that spoil our lawns.

The white-throated sparrow, a large and very pretty bird, eats the seeds of smartweed and ragweed. Other finches like bittersweet, sorrel, and amaranth, all of which we are glad to have them eat.

The seed-eating birds can find their food in winter, even when snow covers the ground, because the dead weeds hold on to their seeds, and the snow is not often deep enough to cover them.

Some birds gather their food in the fall, and hide it away where they can find it in winter. Blue jays collect acorns and beech-nuts, and store them in a hole in a tree, or some other safe place, to eat when food is scarce. A woodpecker who lives in the West picks holes in the bark of a tree, and puts an acorn into each one.

The oddest store I know of was made by a woodpecker. He found a long crack in a post, and stuffed it full of live grasshoppers. He did not like dead grasshoppers. He wedged them into the crack so tightly that they could not get out, and I do not know that they wanted to. When grasshoppers were scarce in the fields, he came day after day to his queer storehouse, till he had eaten every one.

One of the woodpecker family who lives in Mexico stores nuts and acorns in the stems of plants. These stems are hollow and made in joints like bamboo. The bird cuts a hole at the upper end of a joint, and stuffs it full. When he wants his nuts, he cuts a hole at the lower end of the joint and pulls them out.

I once had a tame blue jay, who was fond of saving what he could not eat, and putting it safely away. The place he seemed to think most secure was somewhere about me, and he would come slyly around me as I sat at work, and try to hide his treasure about my clothes.

When it was a dried currant or bit of bread, I did not care; but when he came on to my shoulder, and tried to tuck a dead meal worm into my hair or between my lips, or a piece of raw beef under a ruffle or in my ear, I had to decline to be used as a storehouse, much to his grief.

He liked to put away other things as well as food. Matches he seemed to think were made for him to hide. His chosen place for them was between the breadths of matting on the floor.

Once he found a parlor match, hunted up a good opening, and put it in. Then he went on, as he always did, to hammer it down so tightly that it would stay. One of the blows of his hard beak struck the lighting end of the match, and it went off with a sharp crack. The noise and the flame which burst out made the bird jump three feet, and scared him nearly out of his senses.

After that I took care to keep the matches out of the way of a bird so fond of hiding things.

FOOTNOTE:

Cooper's and sharp-shinned hawks, and great horned or hoot owl.

XIV

WHERE HE SLEEPS

Most birds sleep on their feet.

You know how a canary goes to sleep, all puffed out like a ball, with his head buried in the feathers of his shoulder. He may stick his bill over behind the top of the wing, but he never "puts his head under his wing," as you have heard.

Sometimes he stands straight up on one leg, with the other drawn up out of sight in his feathers, but more often he sits down on the perch, still resting on his feet. Most wild birds of the perching kind sleep in the same way.

It is only lately that we have begun to find out where birds sleep, because it is dark when they go to bed, and they get up before it is light enough for us to see them.

The only way to catch them in bed is to go out in the evening, and start them up after they have gone to sleep. And this is not very kind to the poor little birds. Some men who are trying to learn about the habits of birds have tried this way, and so have found out some of their sleeping-places.

One thing they have learned is that the nest is not often used for a bed, except for the mother, while she is sitting and keeping her little ones warm.

Robins and orioles, and others, creep into the thick branches of an evergreen tree, close up to the trunk. Some crawl under the edge of a haystack, others into thick vines or thorny bushes. All these are meant for hiding-places, so that beasts which prowl about at night, and like to eat birds, will not find them.

Tree sparrows like to sleep in holes in the ground like little caves. The men who found these cosy little bedrooms think they are places dug out by field mice, and other small animals, for their own use. And when they are left, the birds are glad to take them.

When the weather is cold, some birds sleep under the snow. You may think that would not be very warm, and it is not so warm as a bed in the house with plenty of blankets. But it is much warmer than a perch in a tree, with nothing but leaves to keep off the wind.

While the snow is falling, some birds find it as good as blankets for their use. Grouse, who live on the ground, dive into a snow-bank, and snuggle down quietly, while the snow falls and covers them all over, and keeps the cold wind off. Air comes through the snow, so they do not smother.

Some birds creep into a pile of brush that is covered with snow, and find under the twigs little places like tents, where the snow has been kept out by the twigs, and they sleep there, away from the wind and storm outside.

Water birds find the best sleeping-places on the water, where they float all night like tiny boats. Some of them leave one foot hanging down and paddling a little, while they sleep, to keep from being washed to the shore.

Bob-white and his family sleep in a close circle on the ground, all with their heads turned outward, so that they can see or hear an enemy, whichever way he comes.

Hawks and eagles are said to sleep standing, never sitting on the feet like a canary. Some ducks and geese do even more: they sleep standing on one foot. Woodpeckers and chimney swifts hang themselves up by their claws, using their stiff tail for a brace, as if it were a third leg.

Some birds, like the crows, sleep in great flocks. They agree upon a piece of woods, and all the crows for miles around come there every night. Sometimes thousands sleep in this one bedroom, called a crow roost. Robins do the same, after the young are big enough to fly so far.

AMERICAN ROBIN

Audubon, who has told us so much about birds, once found a hollow tree which was the sleeping-room of chimney swifts. The noise they made going out in the morning was like the roar of a great mill-wheel.

He wanted to see the birds asleep. So in the daytime, when they were away, he had a piece cut out at the foot of the tree, big enough to let him in, and then put back, so the birds would not notice anything unusual.

At night, after the swifts were abed, he took a dark lantern and went in. He turned the light upon them little by little, so as not to startle them. Then he saw the whole inside of the tree full of birds. They were hanging by their claws, side by side, as thick as they could hang. He thought there were as many as twelve thousand in that one bedroom.

XV

HIS TRAVELS

Most of our birds take two long journeys every year, one in the fall to the south, and the other in the spring back to the north. These journeys are called "migrations."

The birds do not go all at once, but in many cases those of a kind who live near each other collect in a flock and travel together. Each species or kind has its own time to go.

23

It might be thought that it is because of the cold that so many birds move to a warmer climate. But it is not so; they are very well dressed to endure cold. Their feather suits are so warm that some of our smallest and weakest birds are able to stay with us, like the chickadee and the golden-crowned kinglet. It is simply because they cannot get food in winter, that they have to go.

The fall travel begins soon after the first of July. The bobolink is one of the first to leave us, though he does not start at once on his long journey. By that time his little folk are full grown, and can take care of themselves, and he is getting on his winter suit, or moulting.

Then some morning all the bobolinks in the country are turned out of their homes in the meadows, by men and horses and mowing-machines, for at that time the long grass is ready to cut.

Then he begins to think about the wild rice which is getting just right to eat. Besides, he likes to take his long journey to South America in an easy way, stopping here and there as he goes. So some morning we miss his cheerful call, and if we go to the meadow we shall not be able to see a single bobolink.

There, too, are the swallows, who eat only small flying insects. As the weather grows cooler, these tiny flies are no longer to be found. So the swallows begin to flock, as it is called. For a few days they will be seen on fences and telegraph wires, chattering and making a great noise, and then some morning they will all be gone.

They spend some time in marshes, and other lonely places, before they at last set out for the south.

As the days grow shorter and cooler, the warblers go. These are the bright-colored little fellows, who live mostly in the tops of trees. Then the orioles and the thrushes and the cuckoos leave us, and most birds who live on insects.

By the time that November comes in, few of them will be left. Birds who can live on seeds and winter berries, such as cedar-berries and partridge-berries, and others, often stay with us,—bluebirds, finches, and sometimes robins.

Many birds take their journey by night. Think of it! Tiny creatures, that all summer go to bed at dark, start off some night, when it seems as if they ought to be asleep, and fly all night in the dark.

When it grows light, they stop in some place where they can feed and rest. And the next night, or two or three nights later, they go on again. So they do till they reach their winter home, hundreds or thousands of miles away.

These night flyers are the timid birds, and those who live in the woods, and do not like to be seen,—thrushes, wrens, vireos, and others. Birds with strong wings, who are used to flying hours every day, and bolder birds, who do not mind being seen, take their journey by daylight.

Most of them stop now and then, a day or two at a time, to feed and rest. They fly very high, and faster than our railroad trains can go.

In the spring the birds take their second long journey, back to their last year's home.

How they know their way on these journeys, men have been for many years trying to find out. They have found that birds travel on regular roads, or routes, that follow the rivers and the shore of the ocean. They can see much better than we can, and even in the night they can see water.

One such road, or highway, is over the harbor of New York. When the statue of Liberty was set up on an island in the harbor a few years ago, it was put in the birds' path.

Usually they fly too high to mind it; but when there is a rain or fog they come much lower, and, sad to say, many of them fly against it and are killed.

We often see strange birds in our city streets and parks, while they are passing through on their migrations, for they sometimes spend several days with us.

A sparrow, who was hurt and unable to fly, was picked up one fall and kept in a house all winter. He was not caged, and he chose for his headquarters and sleeping-place a vase that stood on a shelf.

He went with the family to the table, and made himself very much at home there. He picked out what he wanted to eat and drink, and scolded well if he did not have it.

The thing he liked best was butter, and when he was ready to wipe his bill after eating, as birds do, he found the coat-sleeve of the master soft and nice for the purpose. This pleased the bird better than it did the owner of the sleeve, but he tried in vain to keep the saucy fellow off. If he forgot for an instant to watch the bird, he would dash up, wipe off the butter, and fly away out of the reach of everybody.

In the spring the sparrow left the family, and lived out of doors. But, with the first cold weather of fall, he came back, went to his old vase, and settled himself for the winter again. This he did for several years.

XVI

HIS WINTER HOME

Nearly every bird has two homes, one for winter and one for summer.

We can see why birds leave us and go to a warmer and better place for the winter; but why they do not stay in that country where there is always plenty of food, but choose to come back in the spring to their old home, we do not know.

It may be because they want more room to build nests, and bring up their little ones. Or it may be that they want to come back because they love their old home.

Whatever may be the reason, it is well for us that they do so, for if we had no more birds in the summer than we have in the winter, we should suffer very much from insects. We could not raise fruit, or vegetables, or grain, for insects would eat it all. That is one reason we are so glad that birds come back to us in the spring.

Though so many birds leave us in the fall, they do not all go. A few come to us who have nested farther north, and some who have been with us all summer stay over winter too. These last are called "permanent residents," that is, they stay all the year round.

In the Middle States of the East—New York, Pennsylvania, New Jersey, and Ohio—there are twenty or twenty-five who stay all the year. There are several hawks and owls and woodpeckers, the crow, bob-white, the blue jay, and the meadowlark, and, of the little ones, the goldfinch, in his sober winter coat, his cousin the purple finch, the song sparrow, the nuthatch, and the chickadee.

Besides these "permanent residents," there are ten or twelve who come from the north. The funny little saw-whet owl is one, and the snowflake, who loves to frolic in the snow, is another.

Many of our summer birds stay in the Southern States all winter. Those who can eat seeds and winter berries—for instance, robins and bluebirds, catbirds and sparrows—need not go very far south; and some of them even stay in the State of New York.

Most of our birds who do not eat berries, but must have insects, go farther, some to Florida or the West Indies, others to Central America, and a few even into South America,—except the woodpecker, who gets his insects under the bark of trees.

The summer birds of the Western States nearly all go to Mexico for the winter.

The little birds who stay with us are only those who can eat seeds, as I said, or the eggs and insects to be found in the crevices of the bark on trees. These birds do a great deal of good, for each one destroys thousands of insects before they have come out of the egg. One small chickadee will eat several hundred insect eggs in a day.

These little fellows can almost always find their food, for the snow seldom covers the trunks of the trees; but now and then in the winter we have an ice storm; then the trunks and branches are buried under ice, so that the birds suffer, and perhaps will starve to death.

In such a time it will be kind of you who live in the country to put out food for them. You can give them any table scraps of meat or vegetables, or bread, chopped fine for their tiny mouths, with corn or grain for bigger birds.

What they all like best to eat is suet,—which the butcher will give you,—chopped fine, or, better still, nailed or tied to a branch or a fence, so that they can pick off morsels for themselves. This will make them all very happy; but you must see that the English sparrow does not drive them away, or eat it all himself.

Some persons who live in the country or small towns spread a table every day through the winter for the birds. Many come for food, and they have great pleasure in watching them and studying their ways.

One lady I know who is an invalid, and her greatest happiness in the long cold months, when she cannot go out, is to set her breakfast-table, and watch the guests who come to it.

She lives in the southern part of Ohio, and she has all winter cardinal grosbeaks, or redbirds as she calls them, blue jays, tufted titmice, and others. The cardinals are fine singers, and they sing to her every month in the year.

XVII

HIS FAMILY AND FRIENDS

Many people think that as soon as the young birds of a nest are full grown, and know how to take care of themselves, the family separate, and have no more to do with each other. Some have even said that the old birds push the little ones out of the nest to get rid of them.

All this is a great mistake, and any one who has watched them carefully will say so.

In many cases, when the brood is grown and all have left the nest, the whole family keep together. One who has eyes sharp to see will find everywhere little groups of parents with their young. If the old birds rear more than one brood in a summer, the young ones of the first nest keep together.

I have often seen little parties of young bluebirds or sparrows going about after food on the grass, or on the newly cut hay. Now and then one of the parents would come around as if to see that all was well, and then leave them alone again. When the second brood is ready to go out, the whole family often unite in a small flock. In some cases, where they could be watched, they have been known to stay so all winter. All through July and August, in the New England and Middle States, one may see these pretty little family groups.

Some birds who live and nest by themselves, each pair in its own tree, or bush, or field, come together in larger parties after the young are grown, in a social way. A few do this only at night, in what are called roosts, which I spoke of in a former chapter.

Other birds, when nestlings are out, unite in flocks, and stay so all the time, or through the winter. Our pretty little goldfinch does this.

Most of the birds we see about our homes like to have a tree or bush to themselves for their nest. But there are many birds that live close together all the time. Some, you may say, in small villages,—swallows, for instance. We generally see several swallows flying about together. They make their nests near each other. The barn swallow chooses the beams inside the barn, and there are often three or four or more nests in the same barn.

The eave swallows put their mud cottages in a row, under the eaves outside the barn. One would think they needed to have numbers on their doors, to know which was their own.

There, too, are the common crow blackbirds. They come in the spring in crowds, and when it is time to make nests, they find some grove or clump of trees that suits them, and all of them build their nests close together. Often there are two or three on one tree, like a bird city. There they live and rear their little ones, and it is said they never quarrel.

Then there are the birds who get their food from the sea, such as penguins. These birds live in big cities, of many thousand nests. They go to an island where no people live, and build on the ground, or on rocks, or anywhere.

Sometimes they are so near together one can hardly walk without stepping on them. How each mother can tell her own, it is hard to see. They live very happily together, and if a mother is killed, so that her little ones are left orphans, one of the neighbors will adopt them all, and feed and bring them up with her own.

Some of these birds do not even take the trouble to make a nest. They put the eggs anywhere on the sand or earth.

Some one, Mr. Brehm, I think, tells a pretty story about a certain kind of duck who rears two broods every season. After the ducklings of the first brood have learned to take care of themselves, they go about together, getting their food and sailing on the water in a little party, while their parents are hatching the second brood. But when the younger ones are big enough, they are led to the water, and at once their elder brothers and sisters join them. They all swim around together, the youngest in the middle of the group, where they are protected and fed by the elder brood as well as by the parents, a lovely and united little family.

XVIII

HIS KINDNESS TO OTHERS

Birds are helpful to each other when in trouble. If a robin is in distress, other robins will come to see what is the matter, and to help if they can. And not only robins, but catbirds, and orioles, and chickadees, and others, will come, too.

Sometimes when a person tries to rob a nest, all the birds near will come in a crowd, to drive away the thief. They will cry and scream at him, and sometimes fly at his face, and try to peck his eyes.

Birds are so little they cannot fight a man, but if they can peck at his face, they can hurt him, and if they really get at his eyes, they can put them out. We cannot blame the birds for trying to protect themselves and their young, and it is well for boys to be careful how they disturb a nest.

One proof that birds really do help each other is the fact that when a man wants to know what birds live in a place, he can bring them all around him by making a sound like a young bird in distress. All who hear it will come to see what is the matter.

Let me tell you a story of some young swallows. They were able to fly a little, and were sitting together on a roof, when a lady who was watching them noticed that one of them seemed to be weak, and not able to stand up.

When the parents came with food, the others stood up and opened their mouths, and so were fed, but this little one hardly ever got a morsel.

If birds had no love for each other, as many people think, these strong little ones would not have cared if their brother did starve; but what did the lady see? She says that two of the strong young swallows came close up to their weak brother, one on each side. They put their beaks under his breast and lifted him up on to his legs, and then crowded so close against him that their little bodies propped him up, and held him there; so that he had his chance of being fed as well as they.

Many times birds have been seen who were blind or old, or who had a wing or a leg broken, or were in some way hurt so that they could not take care of themselves, and who were being waited upon by other birds, fed, and led to the water to drink and bathe.

CHEWINK, OR TOWHEE

Birds have been found caught in the lining of a nest, so that they were held there and could not go for food. They had been there for weeks, and would have starved to death if they had not been fed. Yet they were so well taken care of by other birds that they were strong and able to fly.

In one case, where the nest was in a tree trunk, the hole in the trunk had grown up, so that when big enough to fly, they could not get out, and they had been there for months. Yet when a man cut open the trunk and let them out, they were well and lively, proving that they had been fed by friends outside all that time.

I could tell you many true stories of the kind care of birds for each other, and for baby birds who had lost their parents, or been stolen away from them.

A gentleman in Massachusetts told me that when he was a boy he saw a small flock of chewinks who came about a house where food was put out for birds. They came every day, and he soon saw that one was bigger than the rest, and that he never tried to pick up anything for himself, but all the others fed him.

One day he was cruel enough to throw a stone at the bird who was so well taken care of, and when he took up his victim, he found that the upper and lower parts of his bill were crossed, so that he could not pick up anything from the ground, where chewinks find their food. He had been born thus deformed, and if he had not been fed every day by his friends he must have starved to death. Yet so well had he been cared for that he was better grown than any of the others.

XIX

HIS AFFECTIONS

I am sure I need not say that father and mother birds love their little ones.

So much does the mother love her nestlings that she is often willing to die for them. Orioles and chickadees will let themselves be caught in the hand of one who has taken their young, rather than desert them.

Some birds live in our chimneys, generally in a flue that is not in use, and are called chimney swifts. If a chimney takes fire the mother swift tries hard to get her little ones out, but if they cannot fly, she has been seen to fly into the fire herself, and die with them.

Robins have been found frozen to death on their nest. They could easily have saved themselves, but they would not leave their young ones to perish. A ground bird has been known to sit on her nest during a freezing storm, till she died, rather than go and leave her little ones to suffer.

Once when a young cedar-bird was caught and carried off, the father followed it for miles, crying and showing so much distress that the man who had stolen it was sorry for him, and let the little one go.

Every one who has watched them knows that birds love their mates. A man once shot a sea bird, when her mate came about him, crying and showing his grief as well as if he could speak.

I could easily fill a book with stories to prove that birds are loving to their mates and young, and all of them true.

It does not seem strange that birds are fond of their own, but they love others also. And not only other birds, but even animals like cats, dogs, and horses sometimes.

I once had an English goldfinch in the house. He was a little fellow, not so big as a canary, and he was very fond of another bird in the room. This was a scarlet tanager, who was much larger than himself.

The small bird showed his love for his red friend, just as people show love, by staying close to him, singing to him, and driving away any bird who came too near.

A lady once told me this story showing the love of a pigeon for a cat. The cat was fond of lying on the broad window sill. When the pigeon saw her there, he would fly down, and alight beside her. Then he would press up close to her, and rub against her fur, as if glad to see her, and the cat seemed to enjoy it as much as the bird.

HOUSE WREN

Often a bird who is tamed loves his human friends. A man had a crow who was very fond of him. He had reared the bird from the nest and never shut him up, but let him fly about wherever he chose.

One day he was out in a sudden rain, and his feathers got wet, so that he could not fly well. Then a boy caught him, and carried him seven miles away. He clipped one wing, so that the crow could not fly, and kept him shut in the house all winter. In the spring, the first time he could get out, the bird started for his old home.

He could not fly, but he walked the seven miles, through mud and wet, and came home so tired that he was almost dead. When his master saw him coming he went to meet him, took him up and petted him, and talked to him.

The poor fellow was so happy it seemed as if he could not live. But he was taken care of, and got well, and lived many years. But never after that would he leave the place, though when his new feathers came in he could fly as well as ever.

Canary birds often love their mistresses. I have heard of one who was so grieved by a harsh word, that in a few minutes he fell off his perch dead.

These true stories show us how tender and loving these little creatures are, and how careful we should be to treat them gently and kindly.

An interesting and true story is told by a clergyman in Ohio. It is a habit of wrens to find a good nesting-place, and then look for a mate to occupy it. One spring a wren chose a nice bird-box on his place, and held it ready for the expected bride. But she did not come, and a pair of English sparrows took a fancy to the same house.

Sparrows expect to get what they want, and are always ready to fight for it, so they gave battle to the wren. But wrens also will fight for their own, and this wren held his house against the enemy for two weeks. Still the mate did not appear, and finally the lonely bird lost heart, and let the sparrows set up house-keeping in his box, though he did not go away.

29

When the young sparrows were hatched, and feeding began, the wren suddenly became friendly. He hunted up small green worms, probably such as are good for wrenlings, and offered them to the young sparrows.

Nestlings are never known to refuse anything to eat, and wren food seemed to suit the sparrows, for they soon outgrew the nursery.

All summer this queer thing went on. The sparrows reared three or four broods, and the wren did his full share of the work,—and not only of feeding the young, but of repairing and rebuilding the nest for each fresh brood.

XX

HIS INTELLIGENCE

Before people knew very much about the ways of birds, it was thought that they did not have to be taught anything, but that they knew everything they needed to know, as soon as they were born. That is, they were said to act from instinct alone, and not at all from reason, as we do.

Another notion that people had was that birds of a kind were just alike; that they looked exactly like each other, all acted in the same way, and all sang the same song.

But since we have begun to study birds more closely, we find these things are not true. We find that birds learn things by being taught, as we do. Also, they find out how to do things themselves, and they are not all alike, as so many machines.

More than this, we see that they do not look nor act exactly like each other. For when we know one robin or one oriole well, we can tell him from any other robin or oriole. And, as I said before, no two of a kind sing precisely the same song.

A bird shows his intelligence in many ways. One is by the way he acts when he cannot do as he is used to doing. A robin I know of wished to build a nest, but could not find mud to put into it, for it was a very dry time, and there were no streams near. Now a robin's nest must have mud, and the bird seemed puzzled for a while. But at last she thought of a way to get it.

She went to a bathing-dish that the people of the house kept filled with water for the birds, jumped into it, and got her legs very wet. Then she flew to the road, and tramped around in the dust and dirt.

In a short time her legs had a good coating of mud, which she carefully picked off with her bill, and took to the nest she was building.

This she did a great many times, and the lady who told me of it watched her till she had as much mud as she needed.

A bird often shows sense by the way she repairs a nest that has been thrown out of place. Sometimes she will add a new stay, tying the nest to a stronger limb. One sparrow, whose nest broke loose, put so many stays to the branch above that they made a little roof like a tent over it.

Another way a bird shows reason is in seeing the advantage of a new place. A pair of swallows lived far out in the West, hundreds of miles from any house. They had no doubt always nested in a cave, or a hole in a tree. But one day they found a house put up. It was a mere shed, to be used as a blacksmith shop, by a party of men who were looking over the country.

At once the birds saw how nice it would be to have a roof over their heads. And although there was a big fire, and the noise of men at work, they built the nest over the anvil, and reared the family in safety.

Woodpeckers have shown that they can learn. Some of them have found an easier way to get food than to dig through the bark of trees for it.

The flicker, or golden-winged woodpecker, has learned that ants and other insects are good to eat, and now he does not think of digging into bark any more.

The red-headed woodpecker has learned to catch flies like a common flycatcher. The yellow-bellied, or sapsucker, cuts holes in the trees, and eats the insects that come to feed on the sweet sap that drips from them.

FLICKER

Woodpeckers have also learned to cut a hole through a board and nest inside a building, instead of drilling a deep hole in the trunk of a tree for a nest.

Birds show intelligence when they draw us away from their young ones, by acting as if they were hurt and not able to fly. I have already spoken about that.

Sometimes when a bird is caught he will lie quiet and pretend to be dead. But all the time he is looking out for a chance to fly away.

A man who watched birds very closely once saw an interesting instance of their intelligence. They were two of the birds who get their food on the seashore by turning over stones and eating the creatures hidden under them. They had found a big dead fish thrown up on the beach and half buried in sand. Under such a fish they were sure they should find food, so they went to work to turn it over. The fish was three and a half feet long, and the birds were about as big as our sandpipers. So it was a hard thing to do.

First they pushed against it with their beaks and breast, but it did not move. Then they went around the other side and scratched away a good deal of sand from under the fish, and went back and tried again to turn it over. Still it was too heavy to stir.

Again they ran around the other side, scraped away more sand, and tried it once more. They kept up this work for half an hour, but did not succeed in stirring the great fish.

At this time the man, who had hidden himself to watch them, saw another bird coming. The two little workers greeted him with joyful cries, to which he replied in the same tones. Then all three set to work on the heavy fish. They dug more sand out from the lower side, and then pushed against the upper side with all their strength. They lifted it a few inches, but it fell back.

At last, after resting a few minutes, without moving from their places, they worked it in this way. They rested their breasts on the sand, put their beaks under, and lifted. When the fish was raised several inches, they held it with their beaks and pushed their breasts against it, when over it went, down the little pitch they had made.

They could not stop, and they went with it, but at once came back and found enough to pay them for their hard work.

One who really watches birds to see what they are doing will see many actions that show intelligence and reason.

HOW HE IS MADE

XXI

HIS BODY

Did you ever think how well the bird is made to suit his life? Look at him.

To fit him to move through the air in flying, his shape is the same that men make their boats to move through water. It is sharp in front to cut his way as he goes through, for even the air needs to be cut.

It is narrower toward the back, and as he flies, the feet are drawn up or trail behind, and even the feathers lie backward. All this is so he can go swiftly through the air, and nothing, not even a feather, will hold him back.

To keep his body upright, so that he will not be top-heavy and tip over as he flies, his weight is mostly below the wings.

If we should try to go through the air as fast as a bird goes, we should find it very hard to breathe. But the bird is made for it. When you come to study his anatomy, you will see what a wonderful little creature he is.

He can sing while he is working very hard to fly upward. If you will try to sing while running up a hill, you will see how hard it is to do that.

A bird's head is joined to his neck at one place, something like a hinge. Other animals, like dogs and cats, have two hinges, or places of joining. That is why a bird is able to turn his head around so far that he can look down his own back. No other creature can do so.

Because of this, he is able to dress every feather on his body, and to sleep with his head laid back on his shoulder.

Nearly all birds have some of their bones hollow, and air-sacs, or pockets, under the skin. These sacs they can fill with air and make themselves light, so that those who live in the water cannot sink, but float like a cork.

Men who study the way birds are made do not yet know all the uses of the hollow bones and air-sacs. That is one of the things left for you young folk to find out.

Birds who get their food in marshes, or the edge of the water, have long legs for wading. They have also long necks, so they can pick up food from the ground.

Birds who swim have webs between the toes, that turn their feet into paddles.

Birds have very large gullets. In many cases the gullet leads into a place called the crop, where food is kept before it goes into the stomach. Sometimes the food is made soft in the crop, and then fed to the young ones, as I told you.

Birds have no teeth, yet they eat hard seeds, like acorns and grains of corn. To break these up, and get them ready for the stomach, they have a gizzard, which is a sort of grinding-mill. And to help in the work of grinding they swallow small stones.

One of the wonderful things about birds is the height at which they can live, and not only live, but fly. A man cannot go higher than twenty-two or twenty-three thousand feet, while moving about or exercising, because the air is so rare he cannot breathe. The highest a man was ever known to go and live, it is said, was less than thirty thousand feet, and that was in a balloon, where he did not move.

But birds go a good deal higher than this, and can fly—which is violent exercise—at that height. It is thought by some that the thinness of the air may be the cause of the great speed with which birds fly in that region. But there is still much to be found out about this.

Besides the marvels of flight, birds have other powers almost as strange. Many of them can fly under water with perfect ease, and, more than that, they can, when they wish, sink slowly till nothing is left above water but their beaks, to breathe. And they can stay so as long as they choose, keeping still in one spot, without moving.

A cormorant in a zoölogical garden, who wanted to catch some of the swallows skimming over the pond, sank his body till only his head was out, and held himself there perfectly still.

Birds who are hunted, as geese, have been known to save their lives in that way, by sinking their body under water, leaving in sight only the tip of the bill, which is so small it is not readily seen.

To do such things, birds must be able to make their bodies heavy when they choose, as well as light, which we know they are able to do by filling their air-sacs with air.

There are many things still to be found out about the powers of birds.

XXII

HIS BEAK AND TONGUE

How does a bird get along without a hand? He has to prepare food; to keep his feathers in order; to build the nest; to feed and take care of the young; and sometimes to fight other birds. How can all this be done without a hand?

Fig. 1.

Bill of Oriole.

The beak is the only thing most birds have in place of a hand, and it is wonderful to see how many things they can do with it.

Orioles use it as a needle, in making the nest. With it they weave strips of soft bark or strings, back and forth, in and out, to make the firm pocket they hang on the elm-tree (see Fig. 1).

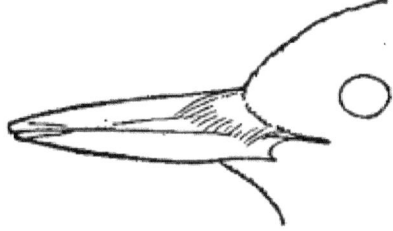

Fig 2.

Bill of Woodpecker.

A woodpecker's beak is a chisel or pick, to cut a deep hole in a tree trunk for a nest (Fig. 2). With a nuthatch it is a hammer, to crack the nut he has wedged into a crevice in the bark so tightly it cannot slip.

WHITE-BREASTED NUTHATCH

Some birds use the beak to dig in the ground, as the bank swallows, while the barn swallows make it a trowel, to carry and plaster mud (Fig 3). All of them use it as a hand to feed themselves, and a brush and comb to dress their feathers.

Fig 3.

Bill of Swallow.

Birds need to use the beak a good deal, because in most cases it grows like our finger-nails. If they did not keep it worn off, it would grow so long as to trouble them. Sometimes when a bird lives in a cage and does not use his bill, it grows so long that he can hardly pick up his food.

The woodcock's long beak is sensitive, so that he can feel the worms, deep in the mud where they live. Many waders and swimmers have beaks soft like leather.

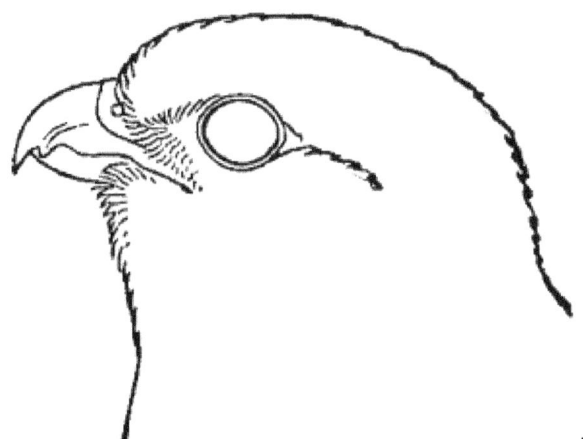

Fig 4.

Bill of Hawk.

You can tell by the shape of the beak how a bird lives, and what he eats. The strong, hooked beak of a hawk shows that he catches live animals to eat (Fig 4). The long, narrow, sharp bill of a heron shows that he spears his prey, often under water.

The sharp-pointed bill of a warbler is to pick tiny insects and eggs out of blossoms, and from under leaves. The sharp-edged bill of a sparrow (Fig. 5) is to break open the hard shells of seeds.

Fig 5.

Bill of Sparrow.

Fig 6. Bill of Crossbill.

The curious beak of a crossbill (Fig 6) is to pick seeds out of pine cones.

A duck's wide beak, with a strainer at the edge, is to let water out while keeping food in. A spoon-shaped bill is to scoop up food, and a thin, flat one is to poke into narrow cracks.

Both parts of the beak, which take the place of our jaws, are called mandibles, upper and lower. Both of them can be moved, while we can move only our lower jaw.

Birds' tongues are as curious as their beaks. To all birds they take the place of a finger, as the beak takes the place of a hand, and they differ as much as the beaks from each other.

Fig 7.

Tip of Tongue of Downy Woodpecker.

Insect eggs are very small, and often packed snugly into cracks and corners, and the birds who eat them have a brush on the tip of the tongue, which brushes an egg out of its hiding-place very easily.

The nuthatch picks his small grubs out of crevices in bark with the four-tined fork at the end of his tongue.

A hummingbird's tongue can be used as a tube, to draw up the honey of flowers, or perhaps as a pair of tweezers, to pick out the tiny spiders that live there.

A woodpecker has barbs on his tongue, to spear insects hidden under the bark, as shown by Mr. Lucas (Fig. 7). It is said to be sticky also, to hold small ones, like ants.

The tongues of birds are of many shapes, but each one is fitted to its owner's way of getting a living.

Because the tongue is often horny, and they eat strange things, it is sometimes thought that birds have little sense of taste. But we cannot be sure of this, and we know they all have notions about their food.

Dr. Ward tells a story of some geese, which shows that they do not lack that sense. While sailing upon a river he noticed on the bank some geese, feeding on the rinds of watermelon, which they picked out of the garbage dumped there.

The rind, when taken out of the mass, was none too clean, being covered with mud and other dirt. When a goose found a piece to suit him, he took it up, carried it to the edge, and dropped it into the shallow water. Then he stood and watched it till the running stream washed it clean, when he stepped into the water and quickly ate off the part he wanted.

XXIII

HIS EYES AND EARS

Birds' eyes are very different from ours. To begin with, they are round. Then they are placed one on each side of the head, so that they can look two ways at once. Owls are the only birds who have eyes turned forward like ours.

Birds' eyes also are of many colors. Besides our common black, brown, blue, and gray, birds have light and dark green, bright red, pale and deep yellow and orange, even white.

They have, like us, two eyelids. But while we use the upper one to close our eyes, most birds use the lower one. They have also a third eyelid, inside the others, a thin, white sort of skin, that moves across the eye from side to side, and is called the "nictitating membrane."

There are other ways in which birds' eyes differ from ours. The men who try to know exactly how birds are made have found out that birds' eyes make everything look much larger than it is, in other words, they are like magnifying glasses, or microscopes, so that a tiny insect egg, that we can hardly see, looks very big to a warbler.

Stranger still, when a bird is far off, his eyes are like telescopes. That is, when a hawk is soaring about far above the earth, he can see a mouse on the ground as well as if he had a telescope to look through. And the gulls who sail about over the shore, and follow steamers on sea voyages, can see small fish and tiny bits of bread thrown out by the passengers, even when they are lost to us in the foam made by the vessel.

Mr. Frank Bolles had a pet barred owl, and used to take him out with him. He says that the bird's sight was wonderful, better than his own aided by a strong glass. Many times the bird would see and watch a hawk so far off that Mr. Bolles with his glass could not see him until he came nearer, and then he looked no bigger than a dot against the sky.

There is a story told of some small birds migrating over the island of Heligoland, suddenly coming down in a flock on to a man's garden, and beginning at once to work among the leaves as if they were feeding.

The owner of the garden knew they did not eat leaves, so he shot a few and found them stuffed with small caterpillars. Then he looked at the plants and found many more caterpillars, each in the curled-up end of a leaf. The insects could not be seen, yet the birds, while flying over, no doubt saw the curled leaves and knew they were there.

Such eyes must be of great use in helping birds to find their food, and to avoid their enemies. But think what giants we must look to them! It is no wonder they are afraid of us.

Perhaps even more useful to a bird than his eyes are his ears, though they are so nicely covered up by the feathers that we cannot see them. The tufts of feathers that stand up on some owls' heads, and are called ears, are not ears at all, but merely decorations, like the crests of some birds and the long tail feathers of others.

But because they cannot be seen, we must not think birds have no ears; they have very good ones indeed. They can hear much better than we can.

Every one has seen a robin run over the grass and turn his head one side to listen. It is supposed that he hears the earthworm move under the sod, and if he is watched, he will often be seen to pull the worm from that very spot.

When a woodpecker taps on a tree trunk and turns his head to listen, it is thought that he hears the grub stir under the bark, for when he begins to cut the bark away, he is pretty sure to find and draw it out.

Birds that are much hunted by men, like ducks and geese, get to be very knowing, and show how wonderful is their hearing. They can tell the difference between a noise made by an animal and that made by a man. A deer or any animal may crash through the bushes, and they pay no attention to it, but if a man makes the least sound they are off in an instant.

A bird's ears are behind the eyes, and a little below them. They are covered by delicate feathers that hide them from sight. When the bird raises these feathers—perhaps to hear better—they look like tiny ear muffs.

Owls have little flaps of skin with which they can shut up their ears when they wish to be quiet. This must be very useful to birds who prefer to sleep during the day, when nearly everybody else is awake and making a noise. Many of us who live in cities would like to be able to close our ears sometimes.

Mr. Bolles tells a story about the sharp hearing of a heron. The bird was on a tree dressing his plumage, and he was hidden in some bushes and could not be seen.

Mr. Bolles made all sorts of noises to start up the heron and make him fly. First he imitated animal sounds. He quacked, and barked, and mewed, and brayed, and the bird looked interested, but not at all alarmed. Then he whistled and sang, and at last talked plainly, but the bird only looked over his way, as if to see what new sort of beast was hidden there.

No noise that he could make startled the heron in the least, until a twig snapped under his foot, when the bird was off like a shot. That sound he well knew was made by his most feared enemy, man.

XXIV

HIS FEET AND LEGS

A bird always stands on his toes, not on his whole foot, as we do. The long slim part that we call the leg is really the foot, and the joint we see nearly up to the bird's body is the bird's heel. But in this book we will speak of it in the common way, calling the toes the foot, and the part up to the joint the leg.

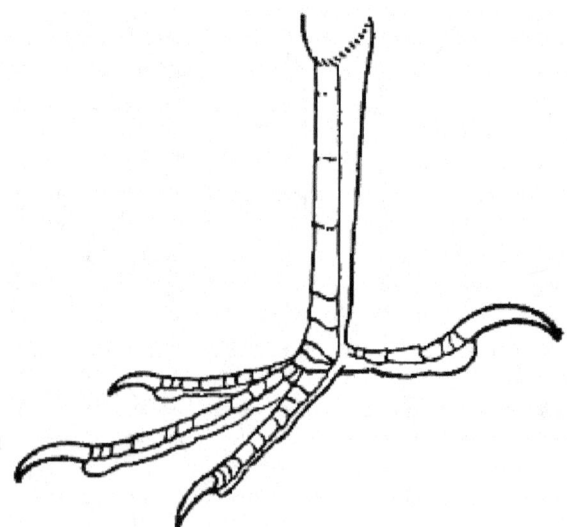

Fig 8.

Foot of Blackbird.

People all over the world have the same kind of feet and the same number of toes; but with birds it is not so. Most of them have four toes (Fig 8), but some have only three, and a few have no more than two.

In the use of the feet there is still more variety. There are, as Dr. Coues divides them, three kinds of feet among birds: —

LESSER YELLOWLEGS

First, a foot that can be used like a hand to clasp a perch, a "perching foot."

Second, one that is good to use as a foot, but not at all like a hand, called a "scratching foot."

Third, one that is like neither hand nor foot, but a paddle, called a "swimming foot."

The birds who have the first kind, the "perching foot," have usually three toes turned forward and one turned back. They can grasp a branch or a twig as tightly as if with a hand, as all our common little birds do. And the large birds of prey, such as hawks and owls (Fig 9), hold in them live mice and squirrels and the other little animals they eat.

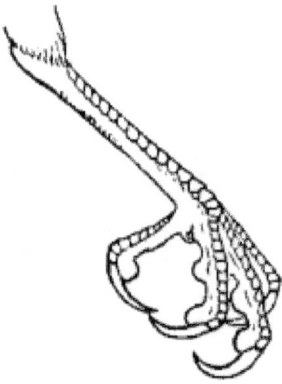

Fig 9.

Foot of Hawk.

Some birds with perching feet have the toes placed another way. Woodpeckers have two turned forward and two turned back, so that they can hold better to a tree trunk (Fig 10).

Fig 10.

Foot of Woodpecker.

A strange thing about the perching toes is the way they are made to hold on, so that the birds can sleep on a perch, and not fall. Inside the toes are tendons, something like cords, which act like elastic rubber. When a bird bends his leg, the toes are drawn up and held so. When he is sitting on a perch, he could not fall off if he wanted to.

Birds who have the "scratching foot," the second kind, mostly go about on the ground, or wade in the water. They do not usually sleep on perches, but sleep standing, or crouch on the ground. In the arctic regions, where there is a great deal of snow, some birds with scratching feet, who have to go about in it, have in winter what has been called "snowshoes," because it enables them to walk on the snow with ease. It is a web-like growth on the side of each toe, which serves the same purpose with birds that snowshoes do with men, keeps them from sinking into the snow.

Birds who have the "swimming foot," the third kind, have the toes made into a paddle by webs stretched between them. They are the water birds,—ducks, geese, gulls, and others.

The toes of all birds have long, sharp claws, not at all like our toe-nails. In the whip-poor-will and the nighthawk, one edge of the middle claw has teeth like a comb.

The long slim part above the toes, what we call the leg, is named in the books the "tarsus." The tarsus is generally bare, with a leathery skin; but in some hawks and owls it is covered with feathers. Birds who live away up in the cold have feathers down on to the toes.

On looking carefully at one of these bare legs, it will be seen that it is not smooth like a lead pencil. It is marked in a sort of pattern. Different species of birds show different patterns. Some look like the shingles on a roof; others like little squares or plates; and some are finer, like scales on a tiny fish.

These marks help in arranging birds in the books. That is, all who have the same pattern are said to be related.

The legs of birds are not all of the same length for their size. Some who never go about on the ground, like hummingbirds, swallows, and swifts, have very short legs. Birds who walk and hop on the ground have them longer, and birds who wade in the water have the longest of all.

XXV

HIS WINGS AND TAIL

A bird's wing does not look much like our arm and hand, yet the bones show that they are the same. The bird has a shoulder, elbow, and wrist, as we have. He even has fingers, though they are so covered up by feathers that one would never know it. He has not so many fingers as we have, and they are not movable like ours.

A bird's wing is a wonderful flying-machine, which men have been trying to imitate these many years. It is made of long stiff feathers, which fold down smoothly over one another at his side when he is resting, but can spread in an instant into a broad fan, to beat the air and carry him away.

One would not think that feathers could have so much power; but when the wing is spread, the barbs of the feathers hook together with tiny hooks, so small a microscope is needed to see them; and that, together with the edges lapping over each other, makes them almost like one solid surface.

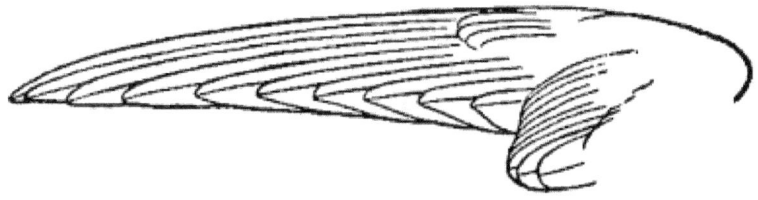

Fig 11.

Wing of Swift.

Wings are not alike in shape. The wing of a swallow is long and narrow, while that of a hen or grouse is short and round. We can tell by the shape of a wing how a bird flies.

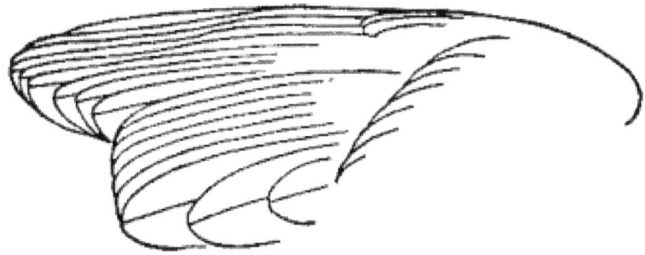

Fig 12.

Wing of Sparrow.

A long, narrow, pointed wing shows that the bird has an easy, skimming flight,—either he flies great distances, or spends hours at a time on wing (Fig 11).

The short round wing (Fig 12) shows that a bird has a strong flight for short distances. These wings are found mostly on rather heavy birds, like grouse.

The longest wings are seen on water birds, such as the petrel and the frigate-bird. The shortest, also, are found among water birds, those who swim more than they fly, as the auks.

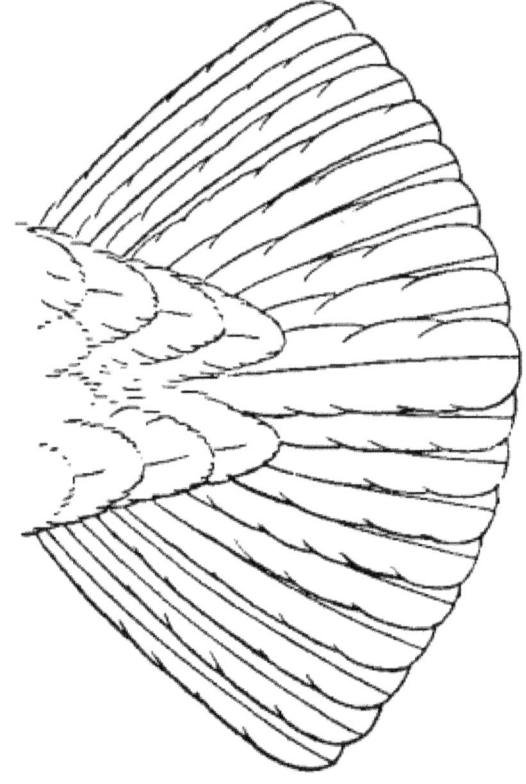

Fig 13.

Tail of Ruffed Grouse.

All the feathers of the wing are named, and it will be well to remember that the long stiff quills are called *remiges* or "rowers." These are firmly rooted in the flesh, and are the hardest to pull out. They are the most important to the safety of the bird.

Birds have also another use for their wings. They are a strong weapon to defend themselves, or to fight others. A large bird can give a severe blow with his wing, and when pigeons fight, it is said they hold up one wing to protect themselves while they strike at the enemy with the other.

Sometimes wings serve as musical instruments. Woodcocks make whistling sounds with their wings as they fly, and mourning doves softly murmuring ones. Ruffed grouse produce with theirs a rolling drum-like effect, and others rattle theirs like castanets.

If wings are not used, they slowly get to be smaller and weaker, each generation having them more and more useless, till after a while they are of no use whatever, and the birds cannot fly at all. This has happened, it is supposed, to the ostrich family and to some birds living in the sea.

BROWN THRASHER

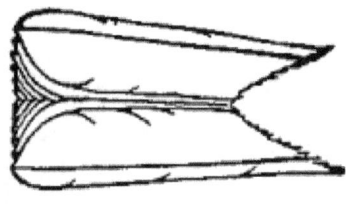

Fig 14.

Tail of Vireo.

The tail of a bird is formed of an equal number of feathers in pairs, most often twelve. When spread they are the shape of a fan (Fig 13), and when closed they lie over each other with the middle pair on top.

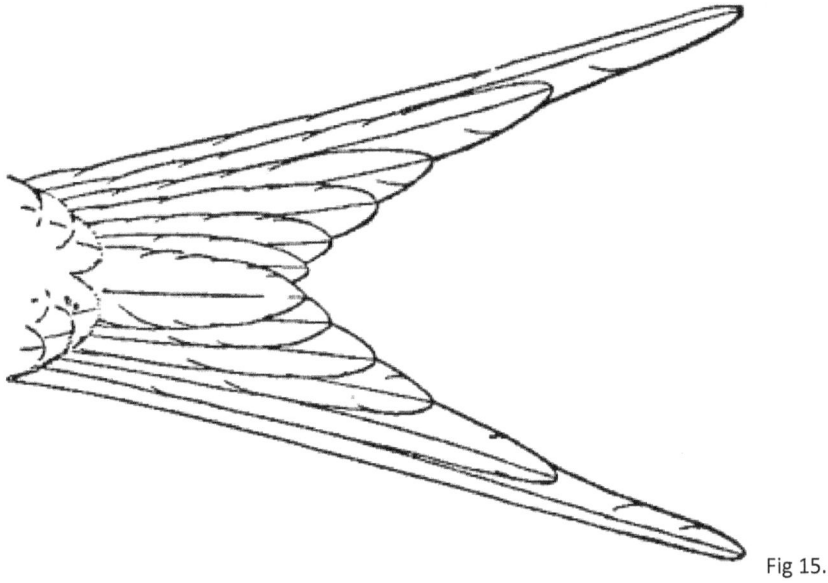

Fig 15.

Tail of Swallow-tailed Kite.

The tail feathers are not always of the same length, and that makes a difference in the shape of the end. Sometimes they are even (like Fig. 14), when the tail is said to be "square." Sometimes the middle feathers are a little longer than the outside ones, and then it is "rounded" or "pointed." If the outside feathers are longest, the tail is "forked" (Fig 15).

The feathers of the tail are called *rectrices*, or "rudders," because they are supposed to be used to steer, or direct the bird's course in flying. But the tail is used also as a brake to check the speed in alighting.

The tail is used more than any other organ to express the emotions. Some birds, like the catbird and thrasher, keep it moving nearly all the time, jerking it this way and that, and tossing it upward.

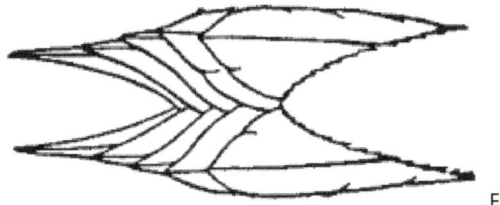

Fig 16.

Tail of Sapsucker.

In woodpeckers and swifts the tail feathers are not soft at the end like others, but the stems or shafts project beyond the feathery part, and are stiff like the tail of a sapsucker (Fig 16) or sharp like this of the chimney swift (Fig. 17). These birds use the tail as a prop to hold them against the tree trunk or chimney wall, and to help them in climbing.

Fig 17.

Swift Tail.

Tail feathers are not so strongly rooted as wing feathers, and are easily pulled out. Sometimes, when a man or boy tries to catch a bird by the tail, the bird will escape, leaving the tail in his hand.

XXVI

HIS DRESS

A bird's whole dress is made of feathers, but the feathers are not all alike. There are, indeed, several kinds of feathers, and four of them are found on every bird. There are flight feathers, clothing feathers, downy feathers, thread feathers, and powder-down feathers.

Feathers of all kinds are made in the same way. All have, first, a quill, the horny part next to the body; second, a shaft, the white part on which the barbs grow; third, the barbs, which grow out on each side of the shaft, and together are called the vane; fourth, the barbules, or little barbs, growing out of the barbs; and last, the barbicels, which grow on the barbules, and on the wings have the tiny hooks which hold them together.

But though feathers are made on the same pattern, they look very different. The wing and tail feathers are stiff and strong, and are called flight feathers, but those on the breast and body are called soft, and cling closely to keep the bird warm and dry. These are called the clothing feathers, because they clothe the bird.

Down feathers, which are almost always hidden under the clothing feathers, are, like their name, downy, and answer to our under-clothes.

Thread feathers grow among the clothing feathers, and are almost like hairs. It is these that the cook singes off the fowls.

Kingfishers who dive, and ducks who spend much time on the water, have very thick down under the feathers—like suits of very warm under-clothes—which keeps the water away from their bodies. Thus they can dive, or sit on the water hours at a time, and not feel wet at all.

Powder-down feathers grow on some herons and cockatoos. They are called by that name because the tip ends are continually breaking off like white dust. Nobody knows their use.

Different from all these are the feathers called plumes, like the long, soft ostrich plumes we all know; the dainty little ones that stand straight up, and look as if the wind would blow them away; the long, showy feathers that the peacock spreads with so much pride, or even the pretty, drooping ones in the cock's tail.

These feathers are of no use for flight or for warmth, they rather hinder than help. They are for ornament, and there are many kinds among birds, all exquisitely beautiful. Nature has given to birds a more wonderful dress than to any other living creature.

It is with his feathers that a bird expresses his feelings. In anger he fluffs them out till he looks twice as big as usual; we have all seen a hen bristle up when a dog comes near her brood.

Nervousness or excitement is shown by jerking the wings and tail, and if a bird wishes to escape notice, he can make his plumage a perfect disguise. Mr. Bolles's pet owl would stretch himself up long and slim, with feathers hugging his body, when he looked so much like a broken branch of a tree that Mr. Bolles could hardly see him. And another owl that I heard of, when he was on the ground, would flatten himself and spread his plumage around, so that the eye could scarcely separate him from the dead leaves about him.

No one takes better care of his dress than a bird, and that is why it looks well for a year. Every day, with most birds, it is washed and carefully dried, each feather being passed through the bill, and the whole thoroughly shaken out. At night one may often see robins and catbirds before going to bed, dressing their plumage and shaking off the day's dust.

Besides washing and drying the feathers, birds need oil to keep them in best condition. For this purpose they have a little "oil jug," a small gland over the tail, out of which, with the bill, they can squeeze a drop of oil. We often see ducks and geese oiling their feathers before a rain.

Water birds, who need a great deal of oil to keep out the wet, have the oil jug very large.

Birds seem to know perfectly well the beauty of their plumage. Not only do they try to show it off, as the peacock when he spreads his tail, but they seem to feel shame when their feathers are injured or soiled. One white feather coming in where it does not belong will make a bird very unhappy. He will work and tug at it to pull it out, and often make himself actually ill over the trouble. I had a captive bird who died, I think, from worry and work over a wing feather which persisted in coming in white, and which he insisted on pulling out every time.

XXVII

DIFFERENT COLORED SUITS

A bird does not always wear the same colored dress, as I said in the chapter on moulting. A goldfinch, who through the summer wears a gay yellow coat, comes out in the fall in plain olive and black; and the scarlet tanager, who flourishes in the most brilliant red, changes to a quiet green in winter. Besides these, some birds wear at one season a spotted coat, and come out afterwards in one of plain colors.

Most of them change by moulting, as I explained, the old feathers dropping out and new ones of another color coming in; or, to speak exactly, the new ones growing out and pushing the old ones off on their tips. But some change color without moulting. All birds moult completely in the autumn, many moult partially in the spring, and some, as I said, change without moulting.

This last change of color is made partly by fading, and partly by breaking off the tips of the feathers, or what is called "abrasion." This is a curious process. I told you something about it in chapter vii. Certain feathers have edges different in color from the rest; as, for example, a black feather with tips of yellow. While the feathers are new and perfect, as they lie over each other like shingles on a roof, only the edges show, and these being yellow, the bird appears to be dressed in yellow. But the yellow tips are not so strong as the rest, and they break or wear off, or are pulled off in the spring. What is strange, they break exactly where the black begins. So as soon as the yellow is off, the black shows, and behold, the yellow bird suddenly becomes a black bird.

That is the way some birds manage to put on their spring dress in the fall. The solid color is the color of the spring, but it is hidden or veiled by tips of another color for winter.

The meadowlark changes in this way. In the winter his coat is brownish, or buff. In the spring these tips are worn or broken off, and he comes out in yellow and black.

Another change, even more curious, is made by some birds, who all winter wear white spots, or light scolloped edges to their feathers, and in spring the spots are gone.

In these, the white or light parts only break off, as sharply as if cut with scissors. They leave the edges of the feathers notched in queer ways, but as they lie over each other that does not show.

BLACK AND WHITE WARBLERS (MALE AND FEMALE)

Birds in this way can change color without changing their feathers. While moulting but once a year, they can show two suits, and by partially moulting twice, can show three suits.

Another thing about the color of feathers is interesting. Some colors, such as black, and red, and brown, are caused by coloring matter in the feather. But other colors are only an effect of the way the feather is made, whether it has ridges on it, or certain minute specks under the surface, which seem to act as prisms (says Dr. Newton), and reflect the light in different colors.

For instance, green is always due to some shade of yellow coloring matter under a surface full of lengthwise ridges, and other colors are made in similar ways.

These curious facts have been found out by that tell-tale little instrument the microscope, and no doubt it will reveal many more secrets in time.

45

Color is useful to birds, as well as beautiful. Its great use is to conceal them from their enemies, and they show that they know this by their conduct.

When a bird is of the color of dead leaves, or the sand, he has only to flatten himself and keep still, and he is hidden. Such a bird on the nest will often let one come close, and even stroke her, while relying on her color to be unseen. A sitting ruffed grouse will do so. But if snow falls, the same bird is very wild, for she knows she can be seen in the snow.

I have seen a striped bird,—black and white warbler,—when frightened, flatten himself on a branch, where he looked so much like the bark that he could not be seen.

Ground birds are mostly in mottled colors of the ground. The whip-poor-will, whose habit it is to rest on a log all day, wears colors that hide him as well as if he were under the log.

The striking colors on a bird are often bidden when he is at rest, but show plainly when he flies. When a flicker stands quietly on a fence he is all in rather dull colors, but when he flies he shows a large snow-white spot on his back, so that as far as one can see him he may be known.

A meadowlark on the ground looks not unlike a flicker, but when he flies he shows that the outside feathers of his tail are white. This is as striking a mark as the white spot on the flicker.

Many birds have such markings, and it is thought by men who study birds and look for a use in everything, that such marks serve the purpose of "danger signals" or "recognition marks." That by these birds can know each other in the dusk, or that the flash of color will catch the eye, when the bird does not wish to give a call, but to slip away quietly to avoid danger, and at the same time to give notice to other birds to do the same.

HIS RELATIONS WITH US

XXVIII

HOW HE WORKS FOR US

Many times in this book I have spoken of the great value of the services of birds, in helping us destroy insects and weeds that injure our crops. But there is more to be said about it.

From morning till night, almost the whole of his life, nearly every bird is working for us. He does not know he is working for us, of course. He is simply hunting for the food he likes, and what is good for young birds to eat.

But what he chooses to eat himself, and to feed the young, consists mostly of creatures that destroy our fruit and vegetables, caterpillars that eat the leaves off our trees, worms that get into our apples and berries, beetles that spoil our roses and our potatoes, mice that eat our crops, and all the worms and grubs that gardeners and farmers are all the time fighting.

As I have already said, some of the birds like cherries and green peas, and other things we prefer to keep for ourselves. But we should never forget that they have earned, by their work among the worms, all they can take.

CEDAR-BIRD

I say this, not merely because I love the birds, and want to have them live and be happy, but because it is true. It has been proved true by scientific men in the service of the United States government.

These men have had thousands of birds killed to see what they were eating, and have found out that nearly all the birds they have examined—blackbirds, cedar-birds, blue jays, hawks, owls, even crows—do us more good by the injurious creatures they destroy, than harm by the fruits and vegetables they eat. To this there is, among the small birds, but one exception, the English sparrow, and, of the large ones, only the two hawks and one owl, mentioned on page 53.

Chickadees like to eat the eggs of cankerworms; and for a single meal, one of these tiny birds will eat two hundred and fifty eggs, and he will take several meals a day. Now cankerworms destroy our apples. When they get into an orchard in force, it looks, as Miss Merriam says, as if it had been burned over.

Robins, catbirds, and shrikes, and several others, like to eat cutworms, which destroy grass and other plants. As many as three hundred of them have been found in the stomach of one robin, of course for one meal. Ants are very troublesome in many ways, and three thousand of them have been taken from the stomach of one flicker.

Rats and mice, ground squirrels and gophers, make great havoc in our crops, and farmers spend much time and labor trying to get rid of them; but these creatures are the favorite food of most hawks and owls.

If the farmer would stop shooting the birds, and protect them instead, they would do this work for him, and much better than he can. But because (as I said in a former chapter) one or two hawks and owls have a taste for chickens, he generally kills every hawk and owl he sees, and for this folly has to spend half his time trying to kill the little animals they would gladly have eaten.

A great deal of refuse, dead sea creatures, and other matter, is thrown up on the seashore, or floats on the water. On this feed the water birds,—herons, gulls, terns, and others. If this were not disposed of, it would make us sick. Indeed, on the shores where so many herons have been killed, to get their plumes for ladies' hats, the result has been sickness and death among the people, as Dr. Gaumer, of Yucatan, told Mr. Chapman.

Besides the work they do for us in destroying animal life, their seed-eating is almost as useful. As I said, they eat the seeds of weeds that farmers and gardeners are all the time laboring to keep down, so that useful plants may have a chance to grow.

The whole family of finches, sparrows, buntings, grosbeaks, and all birds with the high, thick bill, though they eat largely of insects through the summer, and feed their nestlings on them, when insects get scarce and weed seeds are ripe, turn to the latter for food. They eat the seeds of all kinds of troublesome weeds; and as each single seed might produce a plant, we cannot guess how much they destroy.

Professor Beal, who is at the head of this government inquiry into the food of birds, and who knows what he is talking about, says that one species of little bird—the tree sparrow—destroys every year in one of the Western States, many tons of the seeds of weeds.

There is a curious and interesting fact about this seed-eating. The regular seed-eaters, the finches, prefer the seeds of certain weeds, most of them harmful; these they break up, taking off the shells, and of course destroying the germ, making it impossible for them to grow.

But there are many birds who eat berries having in them seeds, such as raspberries, blackberries, and all kinds of wild fruit. These birds do not crack the seeds; and, as they are hard, they do not digest in the stomach, but are dropped whole, and are ready to grow wherever they fall.

Thus, while seed-eating birds destroy the weeds which are hurtful, the fruit-eaters plant the seeds of berries and fruit which we like. That is why we find wild berry bushes all over the country. We have to thank the birds for it.

A great deal more could be said about the birds' work for us, not only of the robins and those I have spoken of, but cedar-birds, who are shot because they take part of our cherries, blackbirds, because they eat some grain, orioles, because they occasionally take green peas, and kingbirds, because they have the name of eating bees, though it has been proved that they eat only drones, which have no sting and make no honey.

Let me impress upon you two facts. First, the stories of the harm done by birds are often mere guesswork, from careless observation. For instance, a man seeing a bird going over his blossoming fruit-trees, at once concludes he is destroying the fruit, probably shoots him, and then writes to his favorite paper that a certain bird eats fruit buds. Other papers copy it, and a war against that bird begins in every orchard.

Whereas, the truth is, the bird was preserving the fruit by picking out the insects that would have spoiled it. This is no fancy picture; this very thing has happened more than once.

And again, whatever is said about the harm this or that bird does, never forget this second fact, which I repeat, and which may be relied upon as perfectly trustworthy. The officers of the government of the United States, who have carefully studied the matter and found out positively, without guesswork, what birds eat, have declared emphatically that every bird they have examined does more good by destroying pests, than harm to our crops, excepting only the bird we have imported,—the English or house sparrow.

XXIX

HOW TO ATTRACT HIM ABOUT OUR HOMES

Because birds are so useful to us, as well as because they are so interesting and so beautiful, it is delightful to have them come about our homes. And it is not at all difficult, for they are easily taught to like us.

In countries where people are gentle, and try to make birds happy, instead of shooting them or throwing stones at them, they become very tame. Mr. Hearn, who has written about Japan, says that the fearlessness of wild creatures is one of the most charming things about the remote parts of Japan, "where tourists with shotguns have not yet come."

Travelers who visit Norway tell us that birds are never disturbed there, and they come freely about the houses. When it is very cold they even come into the houses for food and warmth, and no one thinks of frightening them or trying to catch them.

Even in our own country, Dr. Ridgway told me of a bird-lover in Florida who would not let birds be annoyed on his place. As a result he had a great many there, and they became very tame. Cardinal grosbeaks, who are rather shy, were so tame they would take food from his hand.

A person living in the country, wishing to draw the birds about his place, should begin by protecting it. Cats should not be allowed to come near, English sparrows should be kept down, and boys who shoot or throw stones should be banished from the vicinity.

Next, trees and shrubs that birds like, for nesting and for food, should be set out. For nesting, a very attractive place for the smaller species is a thick hedge of bushes, the thicker and closer the better.

Nesting-boxes nailed up in trees please many, and evergreen trees will draw some that would not come otherwise. For food, various berry-bearing shrubs and trees should be provided, such as chokecherry, shadberry, mulberry, and others.

In a town or city, besides shrubs that birds like, a high fence, with a top that cats cannot walk on, is desirable, and a readiness to go to their assistance is soon appreciated.

A friend told me a few days ago of a family of wood thrushes who nested last summer in the yard of her house in the city of Orange, N. J. The birds soon found out that some of the family would come to drive away strange cats which came in. After they learned that, when a cat appeared they would give a peculiar cry, unlike any other heard from them. On hearing this, one of the family always hurried out and drove the enemy away.

If the birds could not get any response from a call at the kitchen door, they would fly to the front of the house, perch on the piazza rail, and call till some one came out. All through nesting-time they thus called on their friends for protection, and the delight the family had over the nest and the friendly birds amply repaid them for their trouble.

The one great necessity, in both city and country, is water for drinking and bathing. It should be in a shallow dish. The rough saucer of a flower-pot is best, because the bird's feet do not slip on it, and the edge is broad and round and easy to perch on.

Next best is an earthen dish, with clean pebbles in the bottom, to prevent slipping, which frightens them. Water should never be more than two inches deep, but should always be clean, and fresh two or three times a day.

No food should be offered in summer, because we want them to get their natural food of worms and seeds.

In the winter it is different. They should have food regularly. But once used to having their wants supplied, they will depend upon it, and suffer and probably starve, if they are neglected or forgotten. So one should be very sure he will not get tired of it, before he teaches them to expect food.

To feed them safely, a shelf must be placed out of the reach of cats and bad boys. On the sill of a window is a good place, or the roof of a piazza, or a little balcony. Breakfast should be served to them at the same hour every day, and they will soon know when to come for it.

For food, they will eat any table scraps of meat, and vegetables, and bread, chopped fine, and most kinds of grain, broken up, or crushed, for the smaller birds.

But the thing they all like best of everything is raw suet, as it comes from the butcher. A large piece may be wired or nailed in place, so that it may be picked at and not displaced, or it may be chopped fine and scattered on the shelf, like other food. All birds are fond of this.

In winter they need water, and it should then, also, be fresh.

A lady living in southern Ohio, who has for several years given a breakfast to the birds every day in winter, told me that her daily guests last season were hairy and downy woodpeckers, nuthatches, white and red-breasted, one young kinglet, a pair of chickadees, tufted titmice, blue jays, juncos, cardinal grosbeaks, Carolina wrens, and sparrows.

This delightful company came regularly for breakfast, and to pay her, sang nearly through the season.

In the latitude of New York there are about forty birds who spend the winter, and of course there are more as one goes south. In the Southern States, many of our northern birds may be studied in the winter.

XXX

HOW TO STUDY HIM

An attractive thing about bird study is the fact that there is still so much to be found out.

Men have been studying the dead bird for many years. All about the body is well known. The way he is made, the arrangement of his bones and his organs, are plainly set forth in the books, in words and pictures.

The shape and colors of his plumage, how many feathers belong to his wing and tail, his length, his extent, the shape of his beak and his foot,—all these facts are to be found in every Ornithology.

Some of his most easily noted habits, too, are familiar; where and when he nests, where he spends his time, and where he goes in the winter, what he eats, and when he changes his dress.

But really to know the living bird, to make acquaintance with the individual, to see his family life, his manners, his intelligence, his powers,—this kind of study has hardly begun.

This almost new and most attractive field is open to us to-day. It offers a charming study, with the added interest of discoveries to be made. Nor is it so hard as most persons think.

In the beginning there are two things to learn: first, how to study from life; and second, how to identify without killing. To study is simply to observe closely and carefully, and to report accurately.

Take a little lesson in observing: When you see a bird do not merely gaze idly at him, but take note of everything about him. What he is doing, how he is doing it, and all his points, his size and shape, his colors and markings.

If he is getting food, as he most often is, see whether he picks it from the tree trunk or gathers it from grass tops; whether he hunts it among leaves, bores the bark, drops to the ground, or sails out into the air for it.

Then try to discover what it is—insect or seed, beetle, grub, or worm—and what he does with it,—swallow it at once, beat it to death, or hold it in his mouth uneaten.

Then notice his manners,—if he stands still, or jerks his tail or body; if he flits about the branches, hovers before a flower, or hammers at the door of an unlucky grub behind the bark. Next, does he walk or hop? does he chatter or keep silent? fly straight, or go bounding in great waves through the air? All these things you must learn to see, and to note down the moment you do so, so that you will not be uncertain or confused when you take your books to see who he is.

Then you must take note of his size, and to do this—as it is hard to judge of inches—it is well to have in mind a sort of index of size to which you can compare him. Take the most common and best-known birds for standards, the robin, the English sparrow, and one smaller,—the wren, or the "chebec" (least flycatcher). When you see a bird, if he is as big as a robin, enter in your note: "Size, robin." Should he be a little smaller, yet still larger than your measure,—the English sparrow,—you can note it, "Size, robin -," the minus sign meaning that it is less. If he were larger, you would put the plus sign: "Size, robin +."

Observe the shape, whether it is slim like an oriole, or chunky like a chickadee; also any peculiarity of plumage, as a crest, specially long or strangely formed tail feathers; the end of the tail, whether square, rounded, pointed, or notched.

Then notice the beak; its length compared to the head, its shape and color. If it is high and thick, like a canary's or sparrow's, the bird is a seed-eater; if long and straight, like a robin's, he is an insect-eater; if sharp and flat, opening very wide like a swallow's, he is a flycatcher.

Fig 18.

Canadian Warbler.

Lastly, note the plumage, the general color, then special markings, such as bars on wings or tail, a ring around the eye (Fig 18), or a line over or through the eye (Fig 19), white or black throat (Fig 20 or 19), speckled or striped breast (Fig 18), or any conspicuous blotch. Every point must be set down the moment you notice it. You cannot trust your memory.

Fig 19.

Black-throated Green Warbler.

With these full notes, return to your study and take your manual to find out his name, or to identify.

Fig 20.

White-throated Sparrow.

Many persons think that in order to know a bird, and especially to find out his name, one must have him in the hand, count his wing and tail feathers, and measure his length. Excepting for exact scientific purposes, this is not at all necessary. Almost any bird in America may be perfectly identified without touching him, indeed, while he is in the enjoyment of his liberty in a tree. For birds have marked external differences, which are carefully set down in the books.

The modern manuals, too, are usually furnished with a color key, the use of which is fully explained in them. With the help of this you will have little trouble in naming your bird.

Above all, be exact in your knowledge and do not jump at conclusions. If you see a bird on a fruit-tree picking about the blossoms, do not decide offhand that he is spoiling the fruit; look closely to see if he is not, instead, clearing it of worms that would destroy it all. When you notice a bird in a strawberry bed, do not instantly conclude that he is after strawberries; he doesn't care half so much for berries as he does for insects, and very often he is engaged in ridding the plants of pests, at the moment that he is scared off or shot by a careless person, who does not wait to see whether he is friend or foe.

Although patience and clear eyes alone will open many delightful secrets of bird life, a good opera glass will do still more. It will bring you nearer to the bird without frightening him. You can see thus much better, not only his markings, but what he is doing. In a word, you can be more sure of your facts.

In deciding upon the actions of a bird, never *guess* at anything. If you see a pair very busy about a shrub, you may be sure they have a nest there, but do not so record it till you have actually seen the nest. Even then you should not conclude at once that it belongs to them; I have seen birds sit a few moments in nests which did not belong to them—as if to try them. You may feel very sure what a bird means by an action, but you should set down only what he *does*. Without this care, your records will be worthless.

Do not discourage yourself by trying to find the name of every tiny atom in feathers that you see; indeed, little birds flitting about the tree-tops—mostly warblers—will be hard for you to identify, and almost impossible to watch. I advise you to confine your study at first to the larger and less lively birds,—kingbirds, robins, thrushes, phœbes, bluebirds, orioles, goldfinches, and others, all of which you will find near to houses and easy to study. Do not expect too much at once, nor give up in despair if you cannot identify the first bird you see.

SCARLET TANAGER

You may be sure that every hour you honestly give to the study will make it more interesting; every bird you learn to know will be like a new and delightful companion.

You will lose your desire to take life or even to steal eggs from them; the country will have new charms for you; in fact, a person blessed with a love of the study of birds or beasts or insects possesses a lifelong and inexhaustible source of interest and happiness.

In regard to a manual, there are now so many to be had, one hardly knows how to select. I will mention only two or three, which have particular points of value.

A good book to begin with, for residents of New England, New York, and the Eastern Middle States, is Professor Willcox's "Land Birds of New England" (Lothrop Lee & Shepard, Boston. Price 60 cts., by mail).

Although this little book treats of only ninety birds, they are the most common, and its value is its simplicity, and the ease with which its color key enables one to identify the birds it treats. It introduces a beginner to the larger works in a most pleasing way.

A good general work for Eastern North America, thoroughly trustworthy and not too technical in its use of terms, treating all the birds of the locality, is Chapman's "Handbook of the Birds of Eastern North America" (Appleton, New York. Price $3.00). It has a color key and a color chart, by which one may see what is meant by colors named.

Especially attractive to ladies and amateurs, for its charming accounts of bird life, is Mrs. Wright's "Birdcraft" (Macmillan, New York. Price, $2.00). It treats but two hundred species, but that includes the birds usually seen in the New England and Northern Middle States. It has a color key.

The whole United States is covered by Dr. Coues's "Key to North American Birds," 2 volumes (The Page Company, Boston. Price $12.50). It is not quite so easy for the beginner, but it is untechnical in style, and fully illustrated.

One book deserving mention because of its value as an aid to teachers is Miss Merriam's "Birds of Village and Field" (Houghton Mifflin Co., Boston. Price $2.00). It is exceptionally rich in facts and statistics relating to the economic value of birds. It treats nearly two hundred of the most common birds.

A book intended for identification only is Professor Apgar's "Birds of the United States" (American Book Company, New York. Price $2.00). It is the result of his experience as teacher, and has several new features very helpful to beginners, such as small cuts at the bottom of pages to explain terms, thus showing exactly what is meant, for example, by "wing bars" or "rounded tail." It also gives hints about the usual locality of a bird, whether creeping over a tree trunk, on the wing, or elsewhere. It takes particular note of size, having one section for birds about the size of an English sparrow, and so on. The pronunciation of the Latin names is carefully indicated. There are several chapters giving descriptions of the external parts of a bird, and there is a glossary of scientific terms.

The following list of points to observe in watching birds has been used to advantage by classes in bird study. A little familiarity with this will help one to remember what to look for.

A similar, but fuller and more elaborate, list has been prepared, and bound up in tablets, to use in the field. It is for sale by Miss J. A. Clark, 1322 Twelfth Street, N. W., Washington, D. C.

POINTS TO OBSERVE

1. Locality—tree: bush: ground.

2. Size—compared to robin: English sparrow.

3. Form—long: short: slender: plump.

4. Beak—high: stout: wide: hooked: long: lobes: drawn down.

5. Tail—length: shape at end.

6. Legs—long: short: scales.

7. Toes—webbed: how turned: hind claw long.

8. Color—bright: striking: dull: plain.

9. Markings—on head: breast: wing: tail: back.

10. Manners—walk: hop: quiet: active: noisy: silent.

11. Habits—eating seeds: berries: insects: from ground: tree trunk: leaves.

12. Song—long: short: continuous: broken.

13. Flight—direct: undulating: fluttering: labored.

14. Nest—where placed: shape: materials: eggs.

15. Young—plumage: behavior.

SECOND BOOK

THE SECOND BOOK OF BIRDS

I

WHAT IS A BIRD FAMILY?

In the "First Book of Birds" I told you about the common life of a bird; what sort of a home he has, and how he is taken care of when little; then how he lives when grown up; what he eats; where he sleeps; and something about how he is made.

In this book, I want to help you a step further on in your study of birds. I shall tell you something about particular birds, about the families they belong to, and the different ways in which they live.

To begin with: What is a bird family? In life, a bird family is exactly like a human family. It consists of father, mother, and children. But in the books, a family means quite another thing.

Men who study the Science of Birds, or Ornithology, have placed the birds in groups which they call families, to make it easier to find out about them, and write about them. This way of arranging them in books is called classification—or forming them into classes.

Birds are classified, not by the way they look, but by the way they are made, or their structure, and this is found out by the study of Scientific Ornithology. Birds may look a good deal alike, and act alike, and yet be differently made.

There is first the grand class Aves, which includes all creatures who wear feathers. This class is divided into orders.

Orders are made by putting together a large number of birds who are alike in one thing. For instance, all birds who have feet made to clasp a perch, and so are perchers, are put in an order together.

But many birds have feet for perching who are very different in other ways. So orders are divided into families, which I shall tell you about in this book.

In each family I shall tell you about one or more of the best known, or the ones you are most likely to see, and that will help you to know the rest of the family when you begin to study birds out of doors, and use the manual to learn the names.

I shall often speak of what has been found out about the food of birds, and I want to tell you here, once for all, how it was done, so that you may understand just what I mean when I speak of the work of the Department of Agriculture. The Government of the United States has in Washington a department with a head and many men under him, whose business it is to take charge of everything concerning agriculture, that is, farming, fruit-growing, etc. This is called the Department of Agriculture.

Farmers and fruit-growers made so much complaint of the damage done to crops by birds, that this department determined to find out just what birds do eat. The only way it could be done was by having the birds killed and seeing what food was in their stomachs, for it is almost impossible to tell by watching them. To know positively which birds do harm by eating more grain or fruit than insects, and which do good by eating more insects, would save the lives of many thousands. So the killing of those they studied was useful to the whole race.

When they wanted to find out what crows eat, they had crows killed all over the country—hundreds of them—and the stomachs, with the food in, sent to them in Washington. Then they went to work and examined every one. They could tell by the shells of seeds and the hard parts of insects, and bones and hair of mice, etc., just what had been eaten. And the contents of every stomach was written down and preserved in a book. Thus, you see, they could tell what crows were in the habit of feeding upon.

They did this with many other birds who are said to do harm,—hawks, owls, blackbirds, kingbirds, and others. That is how we come to know what birds eat, and can tell whether they do harm or good. There can be no mistake in this way of knowing, and so what comes from this department may be relied upon as true.

I want this little book to help the bird-lovers in the South and West of our big country, as well as in the East; and so, in each Family, I shall try to tell about a bird who may be seen in each part. A good many of our birds are found both East and West, with slight differences, but some that are in one part are not in the other.

II

THE THRUSH FAMILY

(*Turdidæ*)

This family is named after the thrushes, but our familiar robin belongs to it, and also the sweet-voiced bluebird. The birds of this family are all rather good sized, and excepting the bluebird show no bright colors. Nearly all of them have spotted breasts when young, and many of them keep the spots all their lives. Young robins and bluebirds have spots on breasts and shoulders, but when they get their grown-up plumage there are none to be seen.

The thrush family get around by hopping, and do not walk, though some of them run, as you have seen the robin do on the lawn. Most of them live in the woods, and feed on the ground, and all of them eat insects. Because their feeding grounds freeze up in winter, most of these birds go to a warmer climate, or migrate. They are all good singers, and some of them among the best in America.

The best known of this family is the robin, American Robin, to give him his whole name. He is found all over the United States. In the summer he lives in the Eastern and Middle States, in the winter he lives in the Southern States, and he lives all the year round in California.

The California robin is called the Western Robin, and is a little lighter in color than his Eastern brother; but he is the same jolly fellow under his feathers, and robin song is about the same from the Atlantic to the Pacific.

I'm sure you all know how he looks, with black head, slate-colored back and wings, streaked throat, and dull red or chestnut breast. His mate is not quite so dark in color.

Robins start for their nesting-place, which is their real home, very early, almost the first of the birds. They make a nest, not very high, in a tree or about our houses, with a good deal of mud in it. Not all nests are alike. Sometimes a bird will show a fancy for a pretty-looking nest. I have seen one made of the white flowers of life-everlasting. The stems were woven together for the framework, and the little clusters of blossoms left outside for ornament.

The young robin just out of the nest is a pretty fellow, with spots all over his breast and shoulders. He spends most of his time calling for food, for he is always hungry. He is rather clumsy in getting about, and often falls to the ground. But if you pick him up and put him on a low branch out of the reach of cats, he will fly as soon as your hand leaves him, and generally come to the ground again. So it is of no use to try to help him that way. The only thing you can do is to keep cats and bad boys away from him, until he flies up into a tree.

The robin gets his food on the ground, or just under the surface. He eats many caterpillars and grubs that are harmful to us. One that he specially likes is the cutworm, which has a bad way of biting off young plants. In the East he eats many earthworms, which we see him pull out of the ground on the lawn, but in the West, where there are not so many earthworms, he picks up insects of various kinds.

All through spring, when insects are hard at work destroying our fruit and vegetables and young grains, the robin spends almost his whole time catching them; first for his own eating, but many more when his little ones get out of the shell, for young birds eat a great amount of food. Then, when he has spent months in our service killing insects, so that our fruit and vegetables can grow, do you not think he has earned part of the cherries he has saved?

Robins are very easily made tame, and, when well treated and not shut up in a cage, they become fond of people and like to live in our houses. I know of a robin who was picked up from the ground by a lady. He could not fly, and she took him into a house and brought him up. He was never wild or afraid of people, and he never wanted to be free. His mistress would sometimes put him on her hat, without fastening him in any way, and go out to walk with him there. He liked his ride, and never thought of leaving her. She often took him with her into a piece of woods where she went. He would play around on the ground and in the trees, but the moment she started for home he flew down, ready to go.

She thought perhaps he would like to be free, and she tried once or twice to leave him in this pleasant grove, but he always flew to her and refused to be left. He was so fond of his mistress that when she went away for a day or two he was very unhappy, hid himself in a closet, and would not eat till she came back.

This robin, too, liked the food of the family, and did not care for earthworms. In fact, he could hardly be coaxed to eat one of them, though he liked some kinds of grubs which he found on the ground. But he ate them in a different way from his wild brothers. He did not swallow them whole, but beat them to a jelly before trying to eat.

This pet had a sweet, low song of his own. He never sang like his wild brothers until his second year, when he had been out and heard them sing.

A pair of robins that were blown from a nest in a high wind were reared and kept in a large cage by Mrs. Grinnell in California. The first year the singer did not sing, but in the second year a wild mockingbird came to teach him. He would alight on the cage, which hung out of doors, and sing softly a long time, till the robin began to do the same. When he could sing, it was more like a mockingbird than like a robin. The mocker was very fond of his pupil, and used to bring him berries and other wild dainties.

These robins made a nest of things the mistress gave them, and eggs began to appear in it. But as soon as one was laid, one of the birds would jump into the nest and kick and scratch till it was thrown out and broken. They seemed to think the pretty blue eggs were playthings. When the weather grew hot, Bobby, the singer, showed his sense by spending most of his time lying in his bathing-dish, covered with water up to his ears. He would lie there an hour at a time, too comfortable to get out even to eat.

HERMIT THRUSH

Birds who are not brought into the house often become tame when well treated. One family in Michigan had a pair of robins who nested close to the house for fourteen years. It was plain that the birds were the same pair, for they became so friendly that they let any of the family pick up a nestling, and showed no fear. But with other people they were as wild as any robins.

One day a man passing by picked up one of the young birds, who was scrambling about on the ground. At once the parents began loud cries of distress, and all the robins in the neighborhood came to help. They scolded and cried, and flew at the thief who wanted to carry off the baby. One of the family heard the row, and went out and claimed the robin, and the man gave it up. The moment the little one was in the hands of a person they knew, the cries ceased. Not only the parents but the neighbors seemed to understand that the nestling was safe.

The way birds act when brought up by us and not by their parents shows that young birds are taught many things before they are grown up. When living in a house, they are not afraid of cats or people, as wild ones are. They do not usually sing the robin song, nor care for the robin food, and they do not seem to know how to manage a nest. I could tell you many things to prove this.

Another charming member of the Thrush Family is the Hermit Thrush. He is a beautiful bird, smaller than the robin. He is reddish brown on the back, with a white breast spotted with dark brown or black. He has large, full, dark eyes, which look straight at you.

The hermit thrush spends his winters in the Southern States, and his summers in the Northern. But in the far West, where are no cold winters, the hermit does not have to move back and forth. In that part of the country the bird is the Western Hermit Thrush.

This bird is one of our finest singers, and a very shy bird. His home is in the woods, and from there we hear his loud, clear song, morning and evening. Many people think his song is the finest bird-song we have. His ordinary call as he goes about is a kind of "chuck." The Western hermit differs hardly at all. He may be a little smaller, but he is the same delightful singer and lovely character.

The mother hermit makes her nest on the ground, and hides it so well that it is hard to find,—though I'm afraid snakes, and squirrels, and other woods creatures who like eggs to eat find it more often than we do.

Shy as the hermit is, he is an intelligent bird. A mother hermit a few years ago strayed into the grounds of a gentleman in Massachusetts and built a nest under a pine-tree. When she was found, she was at first very much frightened. But the owner of the place was a bird-lover, and gentle and quiet in his ways, and she got so used to him that she let him photograph her many times.

A gentleman, Mr. Owen, once captured a young hermit thrush so lately out of the nest that he could not fly much. He kept him in the house several weeks, and found out many interesting things about young thrushes. One thing he discovered was that the bird has his own notions about food. He ate raw meat and earthworms. But when worms were fed to him that came from a dirty place, he threw them out of his mouth, wiped his beak, and showed great disgust. The worms brought from clean garden earth he ate greedily.

The little captive had his own way of eating a worm. He began by worrying it awhile, and then swallowed it tail first.

He showed his instinct for sleeping high by being very restless at night, till let out of his cage. Then he flew to the highest perch he could find in the room, and roosted for the night.

The bird showed himself friendly and not at all afraid of people. Mr. Owen got so attached to him that when he let him go in the woods he felt as if he had parted with a dear friend.

In the picture you see two hermit thrushes. The upper one is singing, and the lower one looking calmly at you, in the way of these beautiful birds.

FOOTNOTE:

_ See Appendix, 1.

III

THE KINGLET AND GNATCATCHER FAMILY

(*Sylviidæ*)

This family is small in our country. There are only three members of it that we are likely to see. But they are most dainty and lovely birds. They are the two kinglets or little kings, not much bigger than hummingbirds, and the blue-gray gnatcatcher, about as small. They are all fond of living in the tops of tall trees, and they generally get their food and make their pretty nests away out of our reach. So we have to look sharp to see them. It is easier to hear them, for they are fine singers.

The Ruby-crowned Kinglet is a plump little bird in olive-green feathers. Below he is yellowish white, and he has two whitish wing bars. On top of his head is a narrow stripe of bright ruby color. But we see him usually from below, so that is not often noticed. He flits about the upper branches, picking out the smallest insects and insect eggs, and eating them. So he is very useful to us.

RUBY-CROWNED KINGLET

Although this bird is found all over our country, he does not nest with us, except sometimes in the mountains. He goes farther north, beyond the United States. The nests that have been found in the mountains of Colorado and Montana were partly hanging, and very large for such a tiny bird. They were made of soft, fine bark strips, and green moss, and hung to the end of a spruce or pine branch.

But the ruby-crown passes his winters in the Southern States and Mexico, and when he starts for his nesting-home, he begins to sing. As he goes north, he stops a few days or a week in a place, and then is the time to hear his sweet voice. When he sings, you would hardly know him. He raises the red feathers on top of his head so that they stand up like a crown, and change his looks very much. In the picture you can see a little of the ruby stripe.

Not much is known of the habits of these little birds, they are so hard to study. They are found all over the United States, in the Southern States and California in winter, and in the Northern States in spring and fall, when migrating.

The Blue-gray Gnatcatcher is a slim little bird, with a rather long tail. He is bluish gray, with some white and black on head, wings, and tail, and he is grayish white below.

He has a sweet song, but it is so low you have to be very near and very quiet to hear it. He is such a talkative, restless fellow, however, that you often see him when you might not hear the song.

The gnatcatcher is one of the most lively of birds. He bustles about in an eager way that shows everybody where to look for the nest. And when there is no nest, he flits over the tree-tops, catching tiny flying insects, and uttering a queer call that sounds something like the mew of a cat. He does not need to be so quiet as birds who build on the ground or near it, because few can get at the nest. It is too high for snakes and boys, and on branches too light for squirrels or big birds. So he can afford to be as chatty as he pleases.

The nest of this bird is one of the prettiest that is made. It is a little cup, upright on a branch, usually near the end so that it is tossed by the wind. Miss Merriam found a pair of gnatcatchers in California, and watched them through many troubles. Their way of building was by felting. That is, they took fine, soft materials like plant down, and packed it all closely together by poking with the beak and prodding it with the feet.

A gnatcatcher's nest is large for the size of the bird. It must be deep for safety, so that eggs and nestlings will not be thrown out by the wind. Three times, Miss Merriam thinks, the little family she watched had to build their nest. Each time it took more than ten days of hard work.

This pretty little fellow has a long tail, and he keeps it in motion all the time. He jerks it up or down, or twitches it to one side or the other; or he flirts it open and shut like a fan, which shows the white edges and looks very gay.

Dogs and cats, as you know, show how they feel by the way they move the tail. Birds do the same, some much more than others. If you watch the way in which they move their tails, you can learn to tell how a bird feels almost as well as if he could speak to you.

FOOTNOTE:

See Appendix, 2.

IV

THE NUTHATCH AND CHICKADEE FAMILY

(Paridæ)

This is another family of small birds. The nuthatches are lively, restless little creatures. You generally see them scrambling over the trunks of trees, head up or head down, as it happens. They are dressed in sober colors, and spend their lives picking tiny insects out of the crevices of the bark.

The White-breasted Nuthatch is the best known in the East. In California the slender-billed takes his place, being about the same in dress and manners. Both of them, East and West, go about calling "quank, quank." The dress is slate-blue and white, with a white breast, a black cap, and black on wings and tail.

Nuthatches nest in holes, either deserted woodpecker nests or natural holes in trees. If such a place is not to be found, the pair will sometimes dig out a home in a decayed stump for themselves.

It is wonderful to see how easily and quickly a nuthatch will run over the trunk and large branches of a tree. Woodpeckers usually go upward, and brace themselves with their stiff tails. If they want to go down, they back down rather awkwardly. Creepers, who also go over tree trunks, go up only, and they also use their stiff tails for a brace. But the nuthatch goes head up, or down, or sideways, and never uses the short, square tail in the business. He can do this because his claws are very curving, almost like hooks, and they grasp tight hold of the little rough places in the bark.

It is a funny sight to see a mother nuthatch going about with four or five hungry little ones after her, like chickens after a hen, all calling their droll little "quanks."

The nuthatch gets his name, it is said, from the habit of fixing a nut into a crack and hammering or "hacking" it till it breaks. In summer, when insects are to be had, this bird, like many others, eats nothing else, and he eats thousands of them. But he can live on other food, so he is not forced to migrate.

To provide for winter, when insects will be gone and snow cover the seeds, he lays up a store of food. He takes kernels of corn, if he can get them, or sunflower seeds, or nuts of various kinds. This keeps him very busy all the fall, and he has often been seen at the work. He will carry a nut to a tree and find a crack in the bark just big enough to hold it. He tries one after another till he finds one to fit. Then he hammers it in till it is secure, and leaves it there. Then in winter the same bird has been seen, when everything was covered with snow, to dig the hidden nuts out of their hiding-places and eat them.

Many birds who do not migrate, but live in the same place the year round, provide for winter in the same way. So do squirrels and other animals. It is pleasant to think that rough-barked trees, and knotholes, and hollows, are filled with food for the hungry birds. And if they had not that supply, they might starve, or be obliged to leave us.

The Red-breasted Nuthatch is a little smaller than the white-breasted, and has a reddish breast. His home is more toward the north, both East and West. He nests in Maine and other Northern States. His call note is different too. It sounds like the squawk of a toy trumpet. His habits are much like those of his bigger relative.

The nuthatch is fond of his mate, and takes good care of her in nesting time. He feeds her and the young till they leave the nest.

Mr. Fowler tells a story of an English nuthatch who is almost the same as one of ours. Some bird-lovers were in the habit of putting nuts on a window-sill for these birds to carry away. One day, to see what they would do, somebody put one in a glass tumbler. The birds saw the nut and tried to get it through the glass, pecking and hammering at it a long time. Finally, one got tired or discouraged and flew up to a perch over the tumbler. Then he happened to look down, and saw the nut inside the glass. Instantly he came down. He alighted on the edge of the tumbler and held on tightly, while he leaned far over inside, almost standing on his head, till he picked up the nut and carried it off.

These birds are easily made tame in winter by feeding them every day when food is hard to get; and at a time when they are forced to live on seeds and nuts, they greatly enjoy scraps of meat, and most of all, suet. Many people put out food for the birds every day in winter, in some safe place where cats cannot come. They have great pleasure in watching their little guests.

BLACK-CAPPED CHICKADEES

Chickadees, or Titmice, as they are named in the books, belong to another branch of this Family. There are a good many titmice in the world, seventy-five kinds or species, but we in America have only thirteen. Best known in the Eastern and Middle States is the common chickadee. In California, the mountain chickadee has habits about the same, and the Southern States have the tufted titmouse.

All these little fellows are pretty birds in gray, set off with black and white, with lovely soft and fluffy plumage.

The common Chickadee and his brother of the West have black on top of the head and on the throat, and white at the side of the head. They nest in holes in a tree or stump. If they can find the old home of a woodpecker, they are glad to get it, but if they cannot find one, they are able to cut one out for themselves, though it is a hard, long job for them.

These birds have very large families, sometimes as many as eight or nine little chickadees in one of those dark nurseries. How so many can live there it is hard to see. They must be all in a heap.

Everybody knows the common call of the chickadee,—"chick-a-dee-dee;" but he has a song, too. It is slow, sad-sounding, and of two notes, almost like the common cry of the phœbe. But you must not think they have no more than these few notes. They have odd little songs, and they make queer sounds that seem much like talking. Almost all birds have many notes and calls and little chatty noises of different sorts, besides their regular song and the common call note. To hear these, and learn to know a bird whatever he says, is one of the delights of bird study. I hope you will some day enjoy it. The Chippewa Indians named the chickadee "kitch-kitch-ga-ne-shi."

A chickadee is a friendly little fellow. Many times one has come down on to a man's hand or knee. Mr. Torrey once found a pair making their nest, and he climbed up on to a branch of the tree, close by where they were working, so as to watch them. Many birds would have been frightened to have a man so near, but not the brave little chickadees. They stared at him a little, but went right on with their building.

These birds, though so tiny, are among the most useful to us, because they spy out and destroy the insect eggs hidden in crevices of bark, or under leaves. Bigger birds might not care to pick up such small things, or their beaks might be too clumsy to get at them.

When you see a chickadee scrambling over a tree, hanging head down with all sorts of antics, he is no doubt hunting out the eggs. These eggs, if left, would hatch out into hungry insects, to eat the leaves or fruit, or to injure and perhaps kill the tree. The nuthatch clears up the trunk and large limbs, and the chickadee does the same for the small branches and around the leaves.

It has been found out that one pair of chickadees with their young will destroy five hundred pests, such as caterpillars, flies, and grubs, every day. No man could do so much, if he gave his whole time to it. Besides, he could not go over the whole tree as a bird does, without doing harm to it. A chickadee hops along the small branches and twigs, looking under every leaf, sometimes hanging head down to see the under side, and picks up every insect or egg. Among his dainties are the eggs of the leaf-rolling caterpillar, the canker-worm, and the apple-tree moth,—all very troublesome creatures.

The Tufted Titmouse is more common in the South and West than his cousin, the chickadee, and he is one of the prettiest of the family. He is dressed in soft gray, with a fine, showy, pointed crest. His ways are something like the chickadee's, but he is, perhaps, even bolder and more pert, and he is easily tamed. All his notes are loud and clear, and he is never for a moment still.

In winter, this bird is found in little flocks of a dozen or more. These are probably all of one family, the parents and their two broods of the year. He is one of the birds who stores up food for a time when food is scarce. In summer, he eats only insects.

The tufted titmouse, like others of his race, has a great deal of curiosity. I have heard of one who came into a house through an open window. It was a female titmouse in search of a good place for a nest. After she had been in all the rooms, and helped herself to whatever she found that was good to eat, she seemed to decide that it was a land of plenty and she would stay.

The stranger settled upon a hanging basket as nice to build in. The family did not disturb her, and she brought in her materials and made her nest. She had even laid two or three eggs, when the people began to take too much interest in her affairs, and the bird thought it best to move to a safer place.

Another of these birds in Ohio, looking about for something nice and soft to line her nest, pitched upon a gentleman's hair. Unfortunately, he had need of the hair himself; but the saucy little titmouse didn't mind that. She alighted on his head, seized a beakful, and then bracing herself on her stout little legs, she actually jerked out the lock, and flew away with it. So well did she like it that she came back for more. The gentleman was a bird-lover, and was pleased to give some of his hair to such a brave little creature.

FOOTNOTE:

 See Appendix, 3.

V

THE CREEPER FAMILY

(*Certhiidæ*)

This is a family of birds who creep; that is, they appear not to hop up a tree trunk like a woodpecker, or walk up like a nuthatch, but they hug close to the bark with claws and tail, and seem really to creep.

The one member of the family in this country is called the Brown Creeper. He is a little fellow in streaks and stripes of brown, and he looks so much like the tree trunks that one can hardly see him. He has a slender, curved bill, just the thing to poke into cracks in the bark, and pull out the insects and eggs hidden there. His tail feathers are curious. They have sharp points on the ends, so that he can press them against the bark, and help support himself.

The creeper's way of getting up a trunk is to begin near the ground, and go round and round the trunk till he reaches the lowest branch. Then he flings himself off, and flies to the roots of another tree, and goes up that in the same way. A brown creeper once came into a house, and found it so comfortable, and food so plentiful, and people so kind, that he stayed. He was very tame, and his great pleasure was to climb up a man's leg or a woman's skirt, exactly as he climbs a tree trunk, going round and round.

BROWN CREEPER

Quiet and demure as he looks, this little bird sometimes plays rather funny pranks. He has been seen to whirl around like a top, and again to fly up and down close to a tree trunk, apparently just for fun. He has a sweet little song, which we do not often hear, for his voice is not strong.

The brown creeper mother takes a droll place for a nest. It is behind the loose bark of an old tree. She makes a snug little home under the bark roof, and lines it with feathers, and there she brings up her three or four little creepers. She is as well protected from sun and rain as if she had an umbrella, and it is such an odd place that it was not for a long time known where her cunning little nest was made.

This bird nests in the Eastern States, in northern New York and New England, and in California he nests in the mountains, but he goes South in winter. When he wants to hide, he makes use of a clever trick, which shows that he knows how much he looks like the trunk of a tree. He simply flattens himself against the bark, and keeps perfectly still. Then you can hardly see him, though you look right at him. You can see in the picture how he looks.

FOOTNOTE:

 See Appendix, 4.

VI

THE CAVE-DWELLING FAMILY

(*Troglodytidæ*)

First Branch

This is a family of singers, who dress in plain colors. There is not a red or blue stripe, and not a yellow or purple feather, among them.

The family has two branches, or subfamilies as the books call them. The first branch, which gives the name to the family, is made of birds who are really a sort of cave-dwellers,—the wrens.

Wrens are lively little birds, excitable and afraid of nothing. They are in plain browns, barred off with another shade of the same color. They are so near the color of the ground, where they spend most of their time, that they are not easily seen. They have a way of holding their tails up, some of them much more than others, by which one may know a wren wherever he sees it.

The most common one of the family is the House Wren. He is found all over the Eastern States. In the Western States the same bird, except in the shade of his coat, is called the Western House Wren.

The house wren is fond of a snug place for a nest. If a wren box is to be had, he will take that; but if not, he will seek some cozy nook, which he will furnish, mostly with fine twigs, and then wait for his mate to appear.

Sometimes the bird takes queer places to live in. I once found a wren family inside a hollow iron hitching-post in a city street. The birds went in through the hole for the hitching-strap. I wondered how the wrenlings would get out through the long, dark passage. Another nest was made in an oriole's hanging cradle, after the young orioles had flown. It was filled up with sticks to make it suitable for baby wrens. One that I found last summer was in a hole in a gate-post.

The place is usually chosen by the male, who stuffs it full of fine twigs, and then sings and calls for his mate to come. He will sing hour after hour his sweet little song, stopping every few minutes to bring another stick to add to his store.

The wren is a droll fellow about one thing,—he never knows when he has enough furniture for his house. He will bring twigs and stuff them into the box or hole, till he can't get another one in. Sometimes even till his mate can't get in herself. A pair began to build in a shed room, and apparently set out to fill the whole room with twigs. They brought in so much stuff that the owner had to stop up the hole they used for a door and make them go somewhere else. He was willing to share the room with them, but he couldn't spare the whole.

The house wren is a plucky little fellow, and as he likes the same kind of places the English sparrow wants, they often quarrel over a box or a nice snug hole. Small as he is, the wren often succeeds in keeping the place he wants, and driving the sparrow away.

English sparrows can be kept out of wren houses by making the opening too small for the bigger bird. An auger hole one inch in diameter will be large enough for wrens, but too small for sparrows. A sparrow has sometimes been seen trying to get into one of these wren boxes, and very droll he looks, when he sticks his head in, and struggles and kicks violently to push himself in.

I found a pair of house wrens in Colorado one summer. The singer spent most of his time scrambling about a pile of brush, apparently trying to make me think that was where he lived. But I was sure he had a mate and a nest somewhere else, and I kept watch for them.

One day I happened to see a little brown bird fly up under the eaves of a summer cottage not much bigger than a tent. On looking closely, I found that there were openings under the eaves. The birds had taken one of these for a door, and built a nest inside, in the box frame over a window. After that I looked at them through another window. Everything went well till the wrenlings left the nest and began to fly around. Then they seemed to lose their wits, or not to mind their parents. They flew wildly about in the cottage, bumping against the glass, and seeming not able to find the door to get out.

I had not the key to open the big door, so I could not help them in their trouble. And the old birds were so frantic when I looked in at the window, while they were trying to get their family out, that I went away and left them. In an hour or two I went back, and found everything quiet, and the wren babies all out on the trees.

FOOTNOTE:

See Appendix, 5.

VII

THE CAVE-DWELLING FAMILY

Second Branch

The second branch of this family is very different from the first; it is composed of mockingbirds, catbirds, and thrashers. These birds were once placed with the thrushes, and by habits and manners they seem to belong there. But, as I told you, families in the bird world are made by structure,—by the way the bird is made. These birds have scales on the leg, and some other things like the wrens, so now they belong to the cave-dwelling family, though they never dwell in caves. They live in shrubbery and low trees. They are larger than any wren, but they are like those birds in being good singers and dressed in plain colors. Wherever they are placed in the books, they are interesting and delightful birds to know.

The most famous of this branch is the Mockingbird, found in the Southern States and California. He is a beautiful and graceful fellow in gray, with large white patches in his wings.

The nest of the mockingbird is a rather rough affair, built in a low tree or a bush. One that I saw was in a tree about as high as an apple-tree. The bird gets his food on the ground, and has a curious habit of lifting his wings as he is about to attack a beetle.

The mockingbird is a celebrated singer. Many persons think him the finest in America. He is especially famous for repeating the notes of other birds; but he can imitate other sounds, such as a policeman's rattle, a postman's whistle, and almost anything else. Sometimes a caged one makes mischief by this accomplishment. He has no need to borrow, for he has a fine song of his own.

Besides being famous in this way, he is a very knowing bird, and a most interesting one to study. The young mocker is a spirited fellow, who can't endure to stay in the nest till his wings are strong enough to bear him. He usually tries to fly too soon, and so comes to the ground. Coming to the ground is a great misfortune to the bird, for he is easily caught and put in a cage.

Being fine singers, mockingbirds are often kept in cages. In the late summer, the bird stores in New York have hundreds of them for sale, birds so young that they still wear the speckled bibs of baby-days. Many of them die, and so every year they are growing more rare.

CATBIRD

A lady wrote me the story of a young mockingbird, whose mother saved it from a cage. The little fellow was just out of the nest, and could not fly far, and a young man thought he would catch him and take him to his sister; but the mother bird wished to save him from such a fate.

When the man went toward the youngster on the ground, the mother flew down, seized him, lifted him up, and flew away with him. She carried him a little way and then let go. He flew as far as he could, but soon came to the ground again. Then the man started for him. Again the anxious mother flew down and lifted him into the air, and again he flew a little and fell to the ground. So it went on for some time, till the young man began to feel ashamed of himself. Then he took up the cage and went away, leaving the little one to his mother's care.

The mockingbird is one of our most knowing birds, and when one is tamed and free in a house, he is very amusing. He is as full of fun as a catbird, and as funny to watch. A true story was told in one of the papers, of a captive who had some queer tricks. One was hunting in a workbox for a paper of needles, taking it down to the floor, and working it open, then suddenly giving it a jerk that sent the needles in a shower all over the floor.

This bird was once shut up in a room alone, while the family were at table. He did not like it, for he wanted to be with them; so he amused himself unwinding all the spools of thread in the workbox. He took one end of the thread and carried it all about the room, around everything and over everything—vases on the shelf, pictures on the wall, chair-legs, sofas, and lamps. Everything in the room was tied together, so that no one could go in lest something should be thrown down. The naughty bird was delighted with his mischief. He sat there singing at the top of his voice. The only way the family could get into the room was to get scissors and cut their way in. They found empty spools all over the floor, and hundreds of yards of thread used.

The Catbird is dressed in plain slate-color. He is a near relative of the mockingbird, and better known in the Eastern States. He is also a fine singer, though he is not so famous. This is partly because he sings usually from the middle of a thick bush and so is not seen, and partly because he does not sing so loud. There is a great charm in the catbird's song.

The catbird is a charming fellow aside from his music. He is as knowing as the mockingbird, and not much afraid of people. He will come near to houses to nest, and if not frightened or disturbed, he will be very familiar.

Like many other birds, the catbird is kind to others in trouble. A pair had a nest near that of a pair of robins. One day the robins disappeared—killed, no doubt—and the young in the nest began to cry. When one of the catbirds came with food for its own nestlings, the robin babies would cry to be fed too. Pretty soon the catbirds began to feed them. And at night, when bird babies need to be covered up by the warm feather-bed of their mother's breast, one of the friendly catbirds filled her place, and kept them warm all night. So it went on till both families were grown up and could fly.

One writer says: "All day long the catbird watches over the fruit-trees, and kills the insects that would destroy them or the fruit. Of course he takes his share, especially of cherries, but for every one he takes, he eats thousands of insects. Where there are no small birds, there will be no fruit." Thirty grasshoppers have been found in one small catbird's stomach by the Department of Agriculture.

A story showing how much the catbird knows and understands is of one in Iowa who had a nest in some vines over a porch. A tornado tore the vines so as to uncover the nest, and the lady of the house feared some one would disturb it. So she began to draw the vines together around it to hide it. While she was doing this, one of the old birds came and began to shriek, and cry, and fly round her head, threatening to dash at her eyes. The mate came too, and acted in the same way, supposing, no doubt, that she was doing some harm to their nest. She shielded her head and finished the work, and went into the house.

The next morning she was sitting on the balcony the other side of the house. All at once a catbird flew down and perched on the railing within six feet of her, which no catbird had ever done before. She kept still, and he began jerking his body and uttering sweet little calls and twitters, turning his head this side and that, with eyes fixed on her. He acted exactly as if he were talking to her, and after a while he broke out with a song, low and very sweet. She sat still, and after the song he began his twittering again, then sang once more. She had never heard anything so beautiful, and she was sure that he was trying to express his thanks to her, and his regrets at the way he had treated her the day before. At least, that was the way it seemed to her.

A catbird is as full of fun and pranks as a mockingbird. He may sometimes be seen to do what looks like playing jokes on others. A lady told me she saw a catbird drive a crow nearly wild by mocking his "caw." He cawed as well as the crow himself, and the crow was furious, dashing down at his small tormentor, and in every way showing anger at what no doubt seemed a great insult.

The Thrasher, or Brown Thrush, is also of this family. He is reddish brown on the back, and heavily spotted on the breast, and he has a long tail which he jerks about a good deal.

He is known all over the Eastern and Southern States, and his California brother is almost exactly like him. He is a fine singer, and has been called the French mockingbird. Sometimes it is hard to tell his song from the mockingbird's.

The thrasher's nest is usually made in a bush, the thickest and thorniest that can be found, and the brave little parents will make a great fight to keep their nestlings from harm. At one time, when a boy went to carry off some young thrashers, the old birds called together quite an army of birds to help defend them. There were at least fifty birds of many kinds, all flying around his head, screaming at him and trying to pick at his eyes. The boy was ashamed, and put back the little ones, glad to get away with his eyes safe.

A Western bird, the Arizona thrasher, builds a nest in the middle of a cactus so full of sharp thorns like fine needles that it is a wonder how the birds can get into it. They pull off the thorns to make a passage, but the nestlings do sometimes get caught and die there. They must, however, be safe from most enemies. One pair that Mr. Palmer tells about built a regular hallway of sticks six or eight inches long.

All the birds of this family have great individuality; that is, no two are alike. The better you know birds, the more you will see that they do not act, or sing, or even look exactly alike. That is one reason why they are so interesting to study.

VIII

THE DIPPER FAMILY

(*Cinclidæ*)

There is only one member of this family in the United States, and that one lives in the Rocky Mountains and the mountains of California. It is the American Dipper, or Water Ouzel.

AMERICAN DIPPER

The body of the ouzel is about as big as a robin's, but looks much smaller, because his very short tail gives him a "chunky" look. His wings are short and rounded, and his plumage is very soft and so thick that he can go under water without getting wet. He is slate-color all over, a little paler on the breast, and his mate is exactly like him, but the young ouzel has all the under feathers tipped with white, and usually a white throat. Both old and young have shining white eyelids which show very plainly among their dark feathers.

The dipper is a water lover. The nest is placed close to it, generally near a waterfall, sometimes even behind a waterfall, where he has to go through a curtain of falling water to reach it. It is on a shelf of rock, and shaped like a little hut, with a hole on one side for a door. It is made of soft green moss, which is kept alive and growing by constant sprinkling. Sometimes the waterfall itself keeps it wet, but the birds have been seen to sprinkle it themselves. They do it by diving into the water, then going to the top of the nest and shaking themselves violently.

This bird is a curious fellow. His food is the small insects which live under water, and he is as much at home there as other birds are in the air. He can walk on the bottom with swift running water over his head, and he can really fly under water, using his wings as he does in the air. I have seen him do it.

The water ouzel cares nothing for the cold. On cold mornings when all other birds sit humped up with feathers puffed out over their feet to keep warm, he is as jolly and lively as ever. He flies about in the snow, dives under the ice, and comes out at an airhole, and sings as if it were summer weather.

Mr. John Muir, who knows so well the Western mountains and the creatures who live there, has told us most of what we know about this bird. He says the ouzel sings all winter, and never minds the weather; also that he never goes far from the stream. If he flies away, he flies close over the brook, and follows all its windings and never goes "across lots."

When the young ouzel is out of the nest and wants to be fed, he stands on a rock and "dips," that is, bends his knees and drops, then stands up straight again. He looks very droll.

Dr. Merriam tells a story which shows how fond the dipper is of water, especially of a sprinkle, and explains why he always chooses to live by a waterfall. The doctor was camping out on the bank of a stream where one of these birds lived, and one morning he threw some water out of a cup. Instantly the bird flew into the little shower as if he liked it. To see if he really wanted to get into the water, the doctor threw out some more. Again the bird flew into it, and as long as he would throw out water, the ouzel would dash in for his sprinkle.

Besides showing that the water ouzel likes water, this little story shows another thing,—that birds are not naturally afraid of us. On far-off islands where men have seldom been, birds do not run away from people. They have not learned to fear them. They will come up to men, perch on their shoulders, and ride with them on their boats. I have read that in Norway, where everybody is kind to birds, they are not at all afraid. They will come into a barn or a house when the weather is cold, or they are hungry, and no man or boy thinks of frightening or hurting them.

Mr. C. Lloyd Morgan has reared many birds by hatching the eggs in an incubator, so that they cannot be taught by their parents. He says that the birds of the wildest parents hatched in that way are never afraid of people who move quietly, or of a cat, or a quiet dog. Any sudden movement startles a young bird, but they are as much afraid of a dead leaf blown by the wind as they are of a hawk. It is the suddenness that alarms them. Some of them stop instantly on a sudden noise, like a sneeze or a cough. If one foot happens to be raised to step, they will hold it so, and if the head is one side, it will stay so, exactly as if they were all turned to stone.

FOOTNOTE:

_ See Appendix, 6.

IX

THE WAGTAIL FAMILY

(*Motacillidæ*)

It does not seem very polite to call a family of birds wagtails, just because they have the habit of jerking their tails as they go about. But that is the name they go by in the books, and we have two of them in the United States. We call them pipits or titlarks.

The best known is Sprague's Pipit, called the Missouri skylark, or sometimes the prairie skylark. This bird gets the name of skylark because he sings while soaring about in the air far over our heads. He could not sing on a tree if he wanted to, for he lives on the plains between the Mississippi River and the Rocky Mountains, where are few or no trees.

SPRAGUE'S PIPIT

The pipits live on the ground, and walk and run, not hop. As they go, they bob their heads, and jerk their tails. They are a little larger than an English sparrow, and they go in flocks. They are never seen in the woods, but in open pastures or plains, or beside a road.

Sprague's Pipit is all in streaks of brown and gray, and lighter below. He has a large foot, which shows that he lives on the ground, and a very long claw on the hind toe.

The nest of the pipit is made by hollowing out a little place in the ground and lining it with fine grasses. Though on the ground, it is one of the hardest to find, because it is lightly covered with the dry grasses, and when the bird is sitting, she matches the grasses so well that one can hardly see her, even when looking right at her.

The birds eat insects and weed seeds, and go about in flocks. Even then they are hard to see, because when they are startled they do not flutter or fly, but crouch or squat at once, and stay perfectly still.

This bird is noted, as I said, for his song. It is said to be as fine as that of the English skylark of which we hear so much. Perhaps his way of singing makes it still more interesting. He starts up on wing, flies a little one way, then the other, all the time going higher and higher. So he climbs on up, up, up, in a zigzag way, till he is fairly out of sight, all the time giving a wonderfully sweet song. It is not very loud, but of such a kind that it is heard when the bird is far out of sight. When he can no longer be seen, one may still follow him with a good field-glass. He will sing without stopping for fifteen or twenty minutes.

Then suddenly he stops, closes his wings, and comes head first towards the ground. It seems as if he would dash his brains out against the earth, but just before he touches, he opens his wings and alights like a feather, almost where he started from. He should be as famous as the English bird, and will be, no doubt, when he is better known.

One of the things which make bird-study so interesting to us is that there is so much to be found out about our birds. European birds have been studied much longer, but we have still many beautiful ones whose manners and ways of living are almost unknown. These things are left for you young folk to find out when you are grown up.

FOOTNOTE:

See Appendix, 7.

X

THE WARBLER FAMILY

(*Mniotiltidæ*)

The gayest, the liveliest, and almost the smallest of our birds are the warblers. Some of them are not over five inches long from the tip of the beak to the end of the tail. Almost all wear bright colors, and the pair are never alike, while the youngsters are different from both.

But few of them warble. Then why are they named so? Well, I haven't found out; but we must call them warblers because that is their name in the books. Most of them have funny little songs of a few notes, which they jerk out every minute as they scramble about on the trees.

We have seventy species of these little birds in the United States, and every one is working as hard as he can from morning till night, for our benefit. For every one eats insects, and enormous numbers of them. Some scramble over trees and pick them out from bud and blossom and under leaves, others go over the bark, and others fly out like flycatchers.

Some of them work in the tops of tall trees, others work in the orchards, some in bushes, and some on the ground. But wherever they live, they are beautiful to look at, and bewitching to study.

Though they are little, they have plenty of spirit. I know of one kept in a room with several other birds, all bigger than himself. You might think he would be treated as big boys would treat a little one. But no, indeed! the tiny fellow made himself ruler of the whole party. He took the biggest bathing-dish, the best seed-cup, and the most desirable perch, and drove away any big bird who dared to claim either.

The Yellow Warbler, found all over the country, is often called the wild canary, for, as you see him fly, he appears to be entirely yellow, but when you get nearer, you will see that on his breast are fine stripes of reddish brown. His mate is all in yellow-olive color.

They are very sweet little creatures, and make one of the prettiest nests in America. It is usually in an upright fork of a tree, or bush. It is made of fine material, among the rest a good deal of a gray silky stuff which gives it a beautiful look.

This bird is one of the few who will not bring up a cowbird baby. When the tiny mother finds a cowbird's egg in her nest, she builds another story on top of the nest, leaving the egg to spoil. Sometimes a cowbird finds the second nest, and then the warbler adds a third story. Nests have been found three stories high, with a dried-up cowbird egg in each of the two lower stories.

A strange thing happened once to a pair of yellow warblers. When the nest was done and the eggs laid, a storm threw it out of place, and tipped it over to one side, so that the little mother did not dare trust it for a cradle. So she built another nest in the same bush, and went to sitting on that.

One day a bird-lover chanced to see the two nests, one with the bird sitting, the other tipped partly over and left with the eggs still in it. To see what the birds would do, he put the fallen nest back in place, and made it firm, and then went away. The little pair looked at the nest, and had a great deal of chatter over it. It was their own nest and their own eggs, but the mother could not sit in two places.

Finally, the singer took his place on the restored nest. After that it was watched, and the two birds sat on the two nests till all the young were hatched, and then fed and reared them. When they were ready to fly, the happy birds had a big family to take care of.

YELLOW-BREASTED CHAT

Besides these tiny fellows that we call warblers, there are four bigger birds classed with the family, who do not look or act like warblers. They are the golden-crowned thrush or oven-bird, the water-thrush, the Louisiana water-thrush, and the yellow-breasted chat.

The Oven-bird gets his name from the nest, which is shaped like an old-fashioned oven. It is on the ground in the woods, often on the side of a little slope. It has a roof over it covered with sticks and leaves like the ground around it, so that it is hard to see.

If you were to see this bird walking about on the ground, as he does, you would think him a thrush. He is something the same color, and he has a speckled breast like a thrush. His mate is dressed in the same way, and they have a dull yellowish stripe over the crown.

He is the fellow you hear in the woods, calling "Teacher! teacher! teacher!" He is found all over the United States east of the Rocky Mountains.

The Yellow-breasted Chat is perhaps the drollest bird in North America. He is a beautiful bird, nearly as large as an oriole, olive green above and brilliant yellow below, and his mate is the same. He is found all over the country south of the latitude of Massachusetts. In the West and California, the chat is a little more gray in color, and has a longer tail. He is called the long-tailed chat, but a chat is the same funny fellow, wherever he is found.

He reminds one of a clown, he plays so many antics, and makes such queer sounds, hardly in the least like a song. He will whistle, bark like a puppy, mew like a cat, or laugh like an old man, all in a loud, strange voice.

Besides this, the chat is a ventriloquist, that is, can make his voice appear to come from some place far off, when he is near, and so fool us. The chat has a way of flying up into the air with wings fluttering and legs dangling as if they were not well fastened on, and looking as if he would fall to pieces himself. He does not like to be seen, either. He prefers to hide in a thick bush, and make all sorts of strange noises to deceive one.

The one thing a chat hates more than anything else is to have his nest found. I have known a chat to desert a nest with three lovely eggs in it, just because it was looked at, though neither nest nor eggs were touched.

I found that nest myself, and I wanted very much to see how the birds live and bring up the little ones, so I was careful not to disturb anything. I hid myself a long way off, where I could see the nest with a field-glass, and where I thought the birds would not notice me. I sat there perfectly still for hours, till the eggs had time to get cold, and I saw another bird carry them off. No doubt they saw me, however, for they never came back to the nest.

FOOTNOTE:

See Appendix, 8.

XI

THE VIREO FAMILY

(Vireonidæ)

The vireos are a small family, fifty species, found only in America. They are very quietly dressed in greenish olive hues, with hardly a bright color among them. They were once called greenlets.

They all live in trees and catch insects, going about over the twigs. They sing as they go, like the warblers, combining work and play. Some of them sing almost without stopping, and it gets to be rather tiresome after a while. One or two of them even sing on the nest, which hardly another bird does.

The vireos make the prettiest nests. They are swinging baskets, hung between the forks of a twig, and usually near the end, where they rock in every breeze. They are not often very high. The birds are easily tamed by one who is quiet, and careful not to frighten them.

YELLOW-THROATED VIREO AND NEST

Mr. Torrey found a vireo on her nest, and by gentle ways got her to let him stroke her. Next day he took some rose leaves with aphides on them, and holding one of the insects on his finger, he offered it to the bird on the nest. She took it, and then another and another, till finally she began to be very eager for them, and he could hardly feed her fast enough. Then he took a teaspoon full of water up to her, and she drank.

Another gentleman—Mr. Hoffmann—did still more. He coaxed a Yellow-throated Vireo till she took food out of his lips. Black ants and cankerworms were the things he fed her. She preferred the ants, and would scold him a little at first when he offered the worms, though she took them at last. This bird was so tame she would let a man lift her off her nest and put her on his shoulder while he looked at the eggs. She would stay there till he put her back.

The yellow-throat, besides making a pretty hanging basket, covers the outside with lichens of different colors, green, dark and light, yellow, and almost black. It is said that these pretty things are put on by the male while his mate is sitting.

A pair was once watched at their building. The female was lining and shaping the inside, and her mate working silky-looking strips from plants into the framework, and then covering the whole with lichens. He was so happy, he sang as he worked.

The one of this family most widely spread over the country, from the Atlantic to the Pacific, is the Warbling Vireo. His song is the most agreeable of the vireo songs, being truly a warble of six or eight notes, of which one does not get tired. The dress of the Western warbling vireo is a little paler, but the habits and manners are about the same as those of his Eastern brother.

72

Vireos were once common in the shade-trees of our city streets, and are still in some places where English sparrows have not taken everything, and boys are not allowed to throw stones or shoot. I know one city in Massachusetts where trees are very lovely and musical with yellow-throats.

We can still have these and other birds in our yards—we who do not live in the middle of a big city—by protecting them from cats and bad boys, and furnishing good places to nest. Mr. Lloyd Morgan tells of a garden near his own where there were fifty-three nests, besides swallows'. The owner planted thick bushes, and some cone-bearing trees. He put bird-boxes and old flower-pots and other things suitable to build in, in convenient places in the trees. The birds appreciated all this and came and stayed with him.

FOOTNOTE:

_ See Appendix, 9.

XII

THE SHRIKE FAMILY

(*Laniidæ*)

A shrike is a pretty gray bird with white and black trimmings. He is nearly as large as a robin, and has a bill slightly hooked on the end. This is to help catch living prey, for he eats mice and other little mammals, besides grasshoppers, crickets, and sometimes small birds.

This family have a curious habit of sticking dead grasshoppers, or mice, or other food, on a thorn, to keep till they are wanted. Because of this habit they have been called butcher-birds.

The Loggerhead Shrike, who is perhaps the most widely known, builds a bulky nest in a tree, and is very attentive to his mate while she is sitting. She looks exactly like him.

He is a very quiet bird, and three or four or more of them may often be seen in a little party together, flying and hopping about in a tree, or on the ground, in the most amiable way. This shrike is a sweet singer, too. The song is not loud, but very pleasing.

LOGGERHEAD SHRIKE

A great deal that is not true has been said about this bird. Some people seem to think he is in the habit of tormenting and killing little birds for fun, and he is called many hard names. But he does not deserve them. His way of keeping his food has been spoken of as if it were a crime. He lives generally on crickets, grasshoppers, meadow mice, and small snakes, besides cut-worms, cankerworms, and many others. He is extremely useful to farmers and cultivators on that account.

Sometimes, when other food is scarce, he eats small birds, but they are by no means his usual food. I have watched a family of shrikes several times, and always looked very sharply to see if they touched birds. I have seen them eat many sorts of insects and grubs, and meadow mice, but never saw one disturb a bird. Other people who have watched them closely have told that their experience was the same. And writers about birds who study for themselves, and do not merely repeat what others have said, generally agree that the bird kills his prey before he impales it. More than that, the number of birds he kills is very small compared to the hosts of troublesome insects and small animals he eats.

The conclusion of the Agricultural Department as to the food of shrikes all over the country is that it consists mainly of grasshoppers, and that the good they do is much greater than the harm, and therefore they should be protected.

Mr. Keyser once saw a shrike catch a meadow mouse, and carry it up into a tree. First he killed it, and then tried to wedge it into a crotch so that he could eat it. But finally he found the sharp end of a broken snag, on which he fastened it.

There is no doubt that the shrike impales his prey so that he can pull it to pieces to eat, for his feet are too small to hold it. I have seen a shrike throw a dead meadow mouse over a fence wire that had sagged to the ground, in order to get bits off to eat.

A lady in New Hampshire who had a captive shrike tells in "Bird-Lore" that he was unable to eat a piece of meat until he could find a place to fasten it. He hopped around the room, looking for something, till she guessed what he wanted. Then she brought a kitchen fork with two tines. The moment he saw it he ran to her, hopped up on her hand, jerked his meat over the tines, and at once began to eat.

An interesting little action of one of these birds was seen by a gentleman traveling in Florida last winter. Wishing to have one of the birds to add to a collection, he shot one (I'm sorry to say). The bird was not killed, but wounded so that he could not fly. As the man came near to pick it up, the poor fellow gave a cry of distress, and fluttered away on his broken wing with great difficulty.

His call for help was heard. Another shrike at once flew down from a tree, and went to his aid. He flew close around him and under him, in some way holding him up as he was about to fall. He helped him so well that the two began to rise in the air, and before the eyes of the surprised hunter, at last got safely into the top of a tall tree, where he left them.

If you ever happen to find a shrike nesting, I hope you will watch the birds for yourself, and see how they act, and not take the word of any one about them. Then you will really know them. The picture shows a shrike as I have often seen one, sitting on the top twig of the tree that holds his nest, watching to see that no harm comes to it.

FOOTNOTE:

_ See Appendix, 10.

XIII

THE WAXWING FAMILY

(*Ampelidæ*)

The waxwings are a family of beautiful birds, with elegant pointed crests, and wonderfully silky plumage. Excepting one species they are in soft grayish or reddish brown colors, with yellow tips to their tails and black lines on the head that look like spectacles, and give them a wise appearance.

Best known is the Cedar Waxwing, or Cedar-bird. He is a citizen at large, you may say, for he is known from sea to sea, and from Canada to Mexico. He nests all over the northern parts, and winters in the southern parts.

This bird gets his name of cedar-bird from the fact that he is fond of cedar berries. He is often called cherry-bird also, because he likes cherries. His name waxwing comes from the little tips like red sealing-wax which are on some of his wing feathers. In Maine he is called the bonnet-bird because of his crest, and in some places he is called silk-tail from his silky plumage. You see he has plenty of names.

Among the strange things about him is that he has almost no voice. The loudest sound he is known to make is a sort of whistle, so low it is like a whisper.

The cedar-bird builds a very neat nest in a tree, and feeds his mate while she is sitting, as well as helps her feed the little folk. The young cedar-bird is a winsome youngster, gentle in his ways, and pretty in his soft gray suit and spotted breast.

One day last summer, a man walking down a quiet road was surprised by a young bird alighting on his shoulder. He walked on home with it, and when he took it off found it was a baby cedar-bird. No doubt he had tried to fly too far and got tired.

The family kept the bird a day or two, and then brought him to me. He was not afraid of anybody, and was perfectly happy so long as some one would keep him warm between two hands.

It was hard to get him to eat, and there were plenty of his grown-up relatives about, probably his own family among them. So I thought it would be safe to put him out. I took him to the woods where I had seen a little family of young cedar-birds, and placed him on a low tree. He brightened up at once, and began to call, and flew to another tree. Fearing that my being there might prevent his mother coming to him, I left him. When I went out again I could not find him, so I hope he was safe with his friends.

I was more certain of it, because I know that these birds are kind to all birds in distress. A lady was once watching a nest of robins when the parents disappeared, no doubt killed. She was much troubled to know how she should get at the high nest to feed the young ones who were calling for their dinner, when she saw a cedar-bird go to them and feed them.

After that she kept close watch, and saw the cedar-bird feed them every day, and take care of the nestlings till they could fly. He no doubt taught them to take care of themselves, but this she could not see, for they flew away.

The ordinary food of this bird is insects that are found on trees, especially among fruit. But they have taken to fly-catching also. A party of them may often be seen busily at work catching flies. This is a very good thing for them as well as for us. The birds or beasts who can eat only one sort of food are called "single-food" animals, and they are growing scarcer every day. They need a change of diet to flourish. We should be sorry to have cedar-birds become scarce.

Cedar-birds are fond of cherries,—as I said,—but they eat hundreds of cankerworms to one cherry. So they earn all they have. Besides, if they can get wild cherries, they prefer them. They have been proved to be among our most useful birds. In one hundred and fifty-two stomachs that were examined, only nine had cultivated cherries.

Cedar-birds eat caterpillars and grubs, and are very fond of the elm-leaf beetle. They have been known to clear the elm-trees of a whole town, where the trees had been stripped for several years before they came. Besides insects, they eat the berries of many wild bushes and trees, such as wild cherry, dogwood, June-berry, elder, and others. They always prefer wild to cultivated berries.

One spring I saw a little flock of cedar-birds in an orchard full of blossoming apple-trees. They spent nearly all their time going over the trees, and working among the blossoms. One who was careless about it might have thought they were destroying apple buds, for they did eat many of the white petals of the flowers. But I wanted to be sure, so I watched carefully with my glass. Then I stayed by that orchard till October, and I never saw trees so loaded with apples as they were. Many branches lay on the ground with their weight of fruit, and in the whole orchard there was but one insect nest. That showed not only that the cedar-birds had done no harm, but that probably they had destroyed thousands of insects that would have done harm.

A bird classed with the waxwings is a California bird, the Phainopepla, or Shining Crested Flycatcher. He is glossy bluish black in color, with large white spots in the wings, which show only when flying. His mate is brownish gray. They are rather slim birds, nearly as big as a catbird.

The phainopepla is a beautiful fellow, with an elegant pointed crest, and plumage shining like satin. He sits up very straight on his perch, but he is a rather shy bird, and so not much is known about his ways. He is a real mountain lover, living on mountains, or in cañons, or the borders of small streams of California, Arizona, and Texas.

As you see by one of his names, he is a flycatcher. Sometimes thirty or forty of them may be seen in a flock, all engaged in catching flies. But like the cedar-bird, he is also fond of berries. When berries are ripe on the pepper-trees, he comes nearer to houses to feast on the beautiful red clusters.

The song of this bird is said to be fine, and like many other birds, he sometimes utters a sweet whisper song.

The nest is placed on a branch, not very high up in a tree, and is often, perhaps always, made of flower stems with the flowers on, with fine strips of bark, grasses, and plant down.

What is curious, and rare among birds, the male phainopepla insists on making the nest himself. He generally allows his mate to come and look on, and greets her with joyous song, but he will not let her touch it till all is done. Sometimes he even drives her away. When all is ready for sitting, he lets her take her share of the work, but even then he appears to sit as much as she. Miss Merriam found a party of these birds on some pepper-trees, and to her we owe most of what we know of their habits.

FOOTNOTE:

_ See Appendix, 11.

XIV

THE SWALLOW FAMILY

(*Hirundinidæ*)

It is very easy to know this family. They are small birds with long pointed wings, always sailing around in the air as if they could never tire. Their beaks are short, but very wide at the head, and the mouth opens as far back as the eyes. They have small and weak feet, so when they alight, it is usually on a small twig or telegraph wire, or on the flat top of a fence or roof.

Swallows wear no gay colors. Nearly all of them look black and white as they sail about in the air. But when you see them closely, you see they are glossy dark blue or green, sometimes with changeable colors, but all dark, on the back.

The Barn Swallow has a dull reddish breast, and his back is rich blue, almost black. He has a deeply forked tail, and a row of white spots on the shorter tail feathers. When he spreads his tail, it is very beautiful.

He is called barn swallow because he prefers a barn for a nesting-place. Up on the beams, close under the roof, the pair build their mud cradle. It is interesting to see them at work. When they have chosen a place, they go to some puddle in the road. They stand around it on their tiny feet, holding their wings straight up like a butterfly's. Then they take up some of the wet earth in their beaks, and work it around till it is made into a little pill. With this pill they fly to the place they have selected, and stick it on to the beam. Then they go back for more. So they go on, till they have built up the walls of the nest, an inch thick, and three or four inches high. Sometimes they put layers of fine grass in, but often they use nothing but mud. Then they line it with feathers which they pick up in the chicken yard.

Some swallows build a platform beside the nest, where one of the pair can rest at night; and when the little ones get big enough to fill up the nest, both parents can sleep there.

When the swallows are flying about low over the grass, looking as if they were at play, they are really catching tiny insects as they go. And when they have nestlings to feed, they collect a mouthful which they make up into a sort of little ball. Then they fly to the nest and feed it to one of the little ones.

Thus they keep the air clear and free from insects, and they do not a bit of harm, for they never touch our fruit or vegetables.

Barn swallows are social, and always go in flocks. They sing, too,—a sweet little song, but not very loud. It is charming to hear them in a barn when five or six of them sing together. But one may often hear the little song from a single bird flying over.

They are friendly among themselves, and they like to alight on a roof and chatter away a long time. In one place where I was staying, they liked to gather on a piazza roof right under my window. They often woke me in the morning with their sweet little voices.

One morning the sound was so near, it seemed as if they must be in the room, and I opened my eyes to see. There on the sill close to the screen was one of the pretty fellows. He was looking in at the open window, and evidently keeping watch of me. When I moved a little, he gave the alarm, and the whole party flew away.

The chatter of barn swallows always seems to me like talk, and men who study bird ways agree that birds have some sort of language. The swallows have many different notes. One is a general warning of danger, but there is another note for a man, another for a cat, and a still different one when they find something good to eat, which they call the others to share.

"The variety of bird speech," says a man who has studied birds a long time, "is very great." And of all bird voices, swallows' are the most like human speech. If you lie on the hay in the barn very quiet, and listen to them when they come in and fly about, you will see that this is true. It seems sometimes as if you could almost make out words.

Swallows more than any other birds like to make use of our buildings for their own homes. Barn swallows take the beams inside the barns, Eave Swallows settle under the eaves outside, and Purple Martins, the largest of the family, choose bird-houses which we put up for them.

It is said that purple martins will not stay anywhere that men have not made houses for them. But I have seen them living in a place not put up for them, though perhaps they thought it was. It was under a terra-cotta covering to a cornice on a business block in the middle of a busy city. The terra-cotta was shaped like a large pipe cut in half, the long way. This half cylinder was laid on top of the brick cornice, and that made a little roof, you see. The whole length of that cornice was thus made into one long room, with a brick floor and terra-cotta roof, and an entrance at the end. That room must have had a dozen martin nests, for a flock was all the time sailing about in the air, above the roofs of the houses.

As these birds eat only flying insects, they cannot stay with us when it is too cool for insects to fly abroad. So they leave us very early. When the little ones are out of the nest and can fly well, swallows from all the country around collect in great flocks, and go to some swamp, or lonely place where people do not go much. There the young ones are taught and exercised every day in flying. And some day we shall go out and find them all gone, not a swallow to be seen. They have started for their winter home, which is far south, in tropical countries, where insects never fail; but it is a comfort to think that next summer we shall have them back with us again.

The swallows I have mentioned, barn swallow, eave swallow, and purple martin, are found all over our country.

Let me tell you a story that shows the purple martin has a good deal of sense. One of these birds built in a box under a window, fixed so that the owner could open it and take out eggs. He took out several, one at a time, and at last he took out one of the birds.

The mate of the stolen bird went off and in a few days came back with another mate. The box was too good to give up, so both the birds went to work to make it safe against the nest robber. They built up a wall of mud before the too handy back door. The egg thief could not get in without breaking down the wall, and he was ashamed to do that. So the birds kept their pleasant home, and reared their family there.

FOOTNOTE:

 See Appendix, 12.

XV

THE TANAGER FAMILY

(*Tanagridæ*)

This is a large family of between three and four hundred species, all dressed in gay colors. But we have only three of them in our country. Their home is in the warmer parts of the world. We have the scarlet tanager in the East, the Louisiana tanager in the West, and the summer tanager in the South. Tanagers are a little larger than sparrows, and live in the trees. They feed on insects and fruit; sometimes, it is said, on flowers.

The Scarlet Tanager is the brilliant red bird with black wings and tail, common all over the Eastern and Middle States. His mate is dressed in modest olive green, and the nestlings are like her the first year.

The tanager himself wears his gay dress only during the nesting season, that is, spring and summer. Towards fall he turns from scarlet to green like his mate, and he is a droll-looking object while he does it. He seems to break out into green patches or streaks. One that I watched began by showing a little green feather among the red on each side of his breast. I have seen one with a green ring around the neck, and all the rest of the plumage scarlet; and another with a green stripe down the back. Some show no regularity about it, but are covered with green patches all over, and look like bunches of colored rags.

SCARLET TANAGER

It is no wonder that a bird hides in the woods, as many do, when changing his coat, if he looks such an object. In spring he gets back his brilliant coat, and comes to our Northern woods again, to nest.

The nest of this bird is not very high in a tree. It is a rather shabby affair, that looks as if it would fall to pieces, and the birds are madly shy about being looked at.

I once saw in the woods a tanager building her nest. I hoped to watch her through nesting, and see how she brought up her little folk. Both of the pair were there, but were too shy to come to the nest while my friend and I were there. We kept very still, and even hid in some bushes, hoping she would not see us. We were so quiet that she was gradually getting over her fright, and coming nearer the nest, when suddenly the big dog we had with us gave a loud sneeze. In an instant both birds were off, as if shot out of a gun. And I think they never came back, for the nest was not finished.

The song of the tanager is much like the robin song, but having once learned it, a sharp ear can easily tell them apart, for it is of a different tone. It is rather hoarse, not so smooth as a robin's voice. The common call is a hoarse and very distinct "chip, chur," given by both of the pair.

Several years ago I saw a scarlet tanager in a bird store. It was winter, and I brought him home to keep till it was safe to set him free in the spring. He was very timid, and did not like to have any one look at him, especially when he went to eat.

If I happened to look at him when he was at his food-dish, he would instantly fly to his top perch, and look as if he would never eat again. So I partitioned off one corner of his cage for a private dining-room, by a strip of stiff paper woven between the wires. After that it was very droll to see him retire behind the screen and eat, now and then sticking up his head to glance over the top, and see if I were looking.

I found it hard to please him with food. He liked living insects, but he wanted to catch them for himself. So I got some sticky fly-paper, and hung it up outside the kitchen door. When I had caught half a dozen flies, I took it up to him. He was not in a cage, and the minute he

78

saw the flies he flew across the room and hovered before me like a big hummingbird, while he daintily picked off every fly. He forgot that he didn't like to have me see him eat. After that I was fly-catcher every day till he learned to like mockingbird food.

In the spring he began to sing—a sweet, low song, different from the common tanager song. Then I took him out to the country, away from the English sparrows, and set him free.

The Summer Tanager nests in the Southern States from New Jersey to Florida. He is all red, but otherwise looks like the scarlet tanager, and his habits are about the same.

The Louisiana Tanager nests in the Western States from the Plains to the Pacific. He is brighter, with a variety of colors. He is mostly bright yellow, with brilliant red head, and black wings and tail, and his mate—like other female tanagers—is in olive green. He is a shy bird, and lives in the woods, and his habits have been very little studied.

I once saw a pair of these birds in Utah, getting their breakfast. At least, the gay singer himself was at that business, though his sharp-eyed mate was too busy watching me to see that I did not mean any harm, to care for food.

They were on a long fence, catching flies. One would fly out a little way, his bill snapping as he seized the fly, and then return to the fence a little farther off. Every time he came back he alighted farther away, though he did not seem even to see me. His mate kept between him and me, and never took her eyes from me. I feared she would go hungry, so I came away and left them.

FOOTNOTE:

_ See Appendix, 13.

XVI

THE SPARROW AND FINCH FAMILY

(*Fringillidæ*)

This is the largest bird family, more than five hundred species, and they are found nearly all over the world. It is divided into sparrows, finches, grosbeaks, and crossbills. All of them are smaller than a robin, and have short, high beaks, with the back corners turned down. The beaks show that they are seed eaters, though all of them eat insects too.

An interesting thing about birds who eat seeds is the grinding machine they have inside to break up the hard seeds. For of course, having no teeth, they are obliged to swallow them nearly whole. What I have called a machine is the gizzard, and you have seen it on the table from a chicken. It is well fitted to grind up the food, and birds often swallow small stones to help in the work.

The first group of this family, the sparrows, are all small, about the size of an English sparrow. They are dressed in dull, brownish colors, more or less streaked, and they live and get their food very largely on or near the ground. Their colors keep them from being easily seen on the ground.

All of this group sing, and some of them are noted songsters, as the song sparrow, the white-throated sparrow, and the fox sparrow. The best known is the little song sparrow, who is found almost everywhere, and is dear to nearly every one.

The Song Sparrow is streaked all over in shades of brown. The breast is white, with the dark brown streaks coming together in an irregular-shaped spot, or sometimes two spots, in front.

The nest of the song sparrow is on the ground or very near it. Sometimes it is in a tuft of grass, sometimes in a low bush a few inches up. One I found at the roots of a little clump of golden-rod, before it bloomed, of course. It was a slight affair, right among the stems, so that it could not be taken up without tearing the plant.

This bird is one of the first to come in the spring, and his song and the robin's are the first we hear. He also stays very late in the fall, and about New York some of them stay all winter. Their food being the seeds of weeds, which are always to be found, they do not need to migrate.

The song sparrow has a sweet and cheery voice, and a variety of songs, and he sings a great deal. I have heard one bird sing six different songs, standing on a fence in plain sight all the time. Some of the songs are charming, and all are pleasant to hear. One never tires of song-sparrow music.

The second branch of this family—the Finches—have some brighter colored members, the goldfinch in brilliant lemon-yellow, and the purple finch in crimson and white.

The Goldfinch, called also the thistle-bird, lettuce-bird, and wild canary, is a charming fellow, dressed, as I said, in lemon color, with black wings and tail and cap. His mate is in olive brown. He is the most delightful of singers, with a sweet voice, and is a common bird all over the country. He flies in great waves, uttering a cheery little warble as he goes over each airy wave.

79

The nest is one of the prettiest we have, in an upright crotch, and furnished with a bed of thistledown an inch thick for the baby goldfinches to rest upon. It is made late in the season, in July and sometimes in August.

One of the most lovely bird-studies I ever had was of a pair of these birds nesting in a low plum-tree. While his mate was sitting, the gay little fellow hung around, doing nothing but watching the tree that held his family. Every little while the sitting bird would begin to call her sweet-voiced "s-w-e-e-t," which sounds so much like a canary's call. On hearing this he would answer her, and at once fly over to see if she was all right, or wanted anything. When he thought it time to eat, he would come and call her off. Both would then go to a patch of weeds, where they cracked and ate the seeds till they had had enough, and then go back to the nursery.

These little birds eat mostly the seeds of weeds,—thistle, ragweed, and beggar's-ticks,—as well as the larvæ of the wheat-midge and other pests, and they feed great quantities to their young.

Goldfinches do not leave us in winter. The male puts off his bright coat and comes out in dull colors like his mate, except that he keeps his black wings and tail. All of a neighborhood collect in small flocks and stay about all winter, looking more like sparrows than goldfinches.

The Western goldfinch which corresponds to this bird is called in California the Willow Goldfinch, but in looks and in habits of life he seems to be the same as the Eastern bird. He is a confiding little creature, and by a person of quiet ways may be made very tame.

Among the finches will be found the Chewink, or Towhee Bunting, a bird nearly of the size of a catbird, who is sometimes called ground robin. He is black and white, with reddish sides and red eyes, and his mate is brown where he is black. He is usually found on the ground, where he gets his food, and where the nest is placed.

There are several species in California, and the Western variety of the common chewink of the East is called the spurred towhee, with habits the same, so far as known.

The chewink has at the best an exquisite song, though there is a great difference in singers, as there is in all bird families. The finest song is like a peal of silver-toned bells.

A bird-lover whom I know found one day a nestling chewink who could not fly much, and seemed to be deserted, or lost, in a barren place on Long Island. Fearing that some cat would get him, he brought the bird home and put him in a cage. The little fellow was not at all frightened at his new surroundings, and became very tame.

The cage of the young bird was near that of an ortolan, a European bird noted as a singer, and a common cage-bird. The baby chewink seemed to take a great liking to the stranger, and tried to do everything he did. Perhaps he felt the need of some education, since he had been deprived of his parents. At any rate, he evidently adopted the ortolan as his model.

When the little one began to sing, he did not sing chewink but ortolan, and he did it so well that one could hardly tell which bird was singing. The gentleman wanted to see if the little fellow would recognize the song of his own family. So he bought a full-grown chewink who was singing, and put him close to his young relative. The new bird was full of music, and sang a great deal. But the youngster paid no attention to him, and kept up his ortolan notes.

This story shows that a bird does not always, if ever, know his native song by instinct, but has to learn it. It is supposed by those who have studied bird ways that he learns it from the old bird before he leaves the nest.

FOOTNOTE:

_ See Appendix, 14.

XVII

THE GROSBEAK BRANCH

(*Fringillidæ*)—Continued

The third division of this family is of grosbeaks. These are the largest of the group, and nearly the size of a robin, with very big beaks. They live in trees and wear some bright colors. They are also fine singers.

In the Eastern States, and west to Missouri, is found the Rose-breasted Grosbeak. He is a beautiful bird, black and white, with a gorgeous rose-colored patch on his white breast, and the same color on the inside of his wings. You can see him in the picture. His mate is modest in stripes of brown and buffy white.

ROSE-BREASTED GROSBEAK

A lady whom I know in New England has had three of these birds living tame in her house, hardly at all confined to a cage. Each one was picked up when just out of the nest and so injured that it could not care for itself. It was carefully fed and reared in the house, and thus saved from death.

One of the three was a female, who was as tame as a domestic cat, and lived in the house four or five years. She was a fine singer, though never a loud one. She kept the family cats in their place by pecking at their toes when they came near, so they had respect for her.

Another was a young singer who had his bill crossed, so that he could not feed himself. He was nearly dead for want of food when he was found. She fed him carefully and brought him up, though she had always to feed him herself. That is a good deal to do, for birds want to be fed very often.

These birds who lived in a house, and were not taught by their parents, never gave the common song of the species, but made up songs of their own. They lived several years with their friend, who was very fond of them.

The rose-breasted grosbeak is one who puts on his gay colors only for the nesting season. When that is over, and he moults, and gets his new winter suit, it is mostly streaked brown like his mate's. The rosy patch is very small, and mixed with brown, so the effect is dull. In the spring he moults the body feathers, and comes out again with his brilliant rose colors.

The bird who takes the place of the rosebreast in the West is the Black-headed Grosbeak. He is reddish brown and black, with the same color and lemon yellow on the under parts, and yellow under the wings, instead of rose like the Eastern bird. He is a loud, enthusiastic singer. Miss Merriam says of him that his song to his mate is finer than that of any other bird she has heard.

The Cardinal Grosbeak, cardinal redbird, Virginia nightingale, or redbird, as he is called in different places, is of the third group of this family. He is found all over the Southern States, and as far north as Southern New England and New York. He is a brilliant red to the tip of his beak, with a beautiful crest and black throat and face. His mate is in soft dove colors, with red beak, and reddish tints on her quiet robe.

Both of the pair are singers. He is much the louder, but she has the sweeter song. He is famous as a singer, and is therefore trapped and caught in great numbers for cages. In Europe, where he is a favorite cage-bird, he is thought by many to be equal to the famous nightingale as a singer.

In Ohio, a few years ago, a law was made that no cardinal should be caged, and those in cages should be set free. In one small village were more than forty freed. This shows how many are caged.

While nesting, the cardinal is rather savage, ready to fight any one who disturbs the nest. If a snake comes about, all the birds within hearing, from cardinals to kinglets, will come to help defend the nest and punish the enemy. They fly at him with loud cries, and even attack him if he does not leave.

The nest of these birds is not very high, in a tree or bush, and they are very shy about it. A cardinal will desert her nest if it is touched, especially if eggs are not yet laid. But they have reason to be afraid; they cannot be blamed for that.

I saw a nest built on a trellis beside a kitchen door, and the birds were so used to the people that they were not afraid. One who lived in that house was a boy fourteen years old. But he was so gentle with birds that they did not fear him at all. They would feed the nestlings freely, while he stood not three feet from them. So they can be made tame, if people will be gentle and not disturb them.

The cardinal grosbeak stays as far north as New Jersey and Ohio all winter, and a little flock have lived in Central Park, New York, for several years. That is most delightful for those who live near, for they sing all winter, when few bird-notes are to be heard. They can stay because they are seed eaters, and they find many weed seeds, and wild berries like cedar berries, that stay on all winter.

CARDINAL

82

A lady once had a cardinal in a cage with a pair of the tiny green parrots called love-birds. These little birds, you know, are always putting the bills together and caressing each other, as if kissing. The cardinal seemed to think this very silly; at any rate, he did not like it. After looking on awhile, he would lose patience and dash right down between them. Of course this drove them apart. Then he seemed to feel better, and went back to his perch. But when they began it again, down he would come between them again. He did not disturb them at any other time, but that sort of thing he plainly couldn't endure.

XVIII

THE CROSSBILL BRANCH

(Fringillidæ)—Continued

The fourth branch of this family is of crossbills. Of these we have two. They are smaller than grosbeaks, and, as their name shows, have the two points of the bill crossed. It looks as if they could not feed themselves. But a beak like this is just fitted to pick seeds out of cones. And crossbills live mostly on cone-seeds.

These queer beaks are used for another thing, too. They help the birds climb around on the trees. They are almost as good as a hand. You have seen a parrot use his beak in the same way.

The American, or Red, Crossbill is the more common of our two. He travels about all over the Northern States and California. But he's very particular about a place to nest, and is suited only in the northern parts, or in the mountains.

The red crossbill seems to be a whimsical fellow; one never knows where to find him. One year he will come with all his friends to a place, and the next year there will not be one there.

The male is dull red, more or less streaked all over with brown. His mate is olive green, mottled and mixed with blackish.

Crossbills go in flocks. They are usually seen among the evergreens, where they find their food. They are much attached to one another.

I had a chance one summer to get well acquainted with a flock of American crossbills. I found them very odd in their manners. They had the queerest songs and calls of any bird I know. These were not musical, but sounded like such things as the squeaking of a wagon wheel or the sawing of wood.

The birds were very fond of calling and singing, and they kept up a constant chattering, as they flew from spruce to spruce. They spent most of their time on these trees, eating the seeds of the cones.

The white-winged crossbill lives about as the red one does. But he has a really fine song. It is full of trills, something like a canary's song.

One of the odd things about these birds is their habit of nesting in winter. A Maine hunter was once shooting moose in the middle of January, when he came upon the nest of a crossbill, with the bird sitting. The weather was cold, of course, and there was deep snow on the ground. The nest was in the woods, and made of twigs, with long gray moss outside. It looked so like a bunch of moss that it was hard to see. Other nests have been found in winter also.

Mr. Nehrling says that if one of these birds is caught, the rest of the flock will not leave him. They stay around him, crying and showing their distress in every way, and if one is put alone into a cage, he will die.

XIX

THE BLACKBIRD FAMILY

(Icteridæ)

There are more than one hundred species of the Blackbird Family in America. So we will divide them into four branches: Marsh Blackbirds, Meadow Starlings, Orioles, and Crow Blackbirds.

RED-WINGED BLACKBIRD

Blackbirds are walkers. They dress mostly in black, and they are of medium size. Some of them will generally be found on the ground in a marsh or a meadow. They are social birds, that is, they go in flocks. Fond as they are of society, however, there is one time when they are willing to be a little apart from the blackbird world. That is when they are nesting and rearing a young family. Two interesting birds of this family are the red-winged blackbird and the cow-blackbird or cowbird.

The Red-winged Blackbird is found all over the country. He is not so large as a robin, and is black all over, excepting one place on the wings. On these are bright stripes of red and orange, which seem to be on the shoulders when the wings are closed. They make the bird very gay, when he spreads them out in flying.

The red-wing's mate is a modest-looking bird in stripes of brown and black. She is a plodding sort of a creature, too. She walks about on the ground, looking for grubs or insects so busily that she hardly seems to see anything else.

The nest is usually in a marsh. At any rate, it must be near the water, for red-wings are as fond of the water as any old sailor. It is hung between reeds, or in the branches of a low bush. It is a comfortable, bag-like affair, deep enough and big enough to hold the restless blackbird babies.

While the mother red-wing is sitting, her mate stays near her and sings a great deal. His song is a loud, sweet "hwa-ker-ee," which may be heard a long way off. When nestlings are out, he is one of the most busy and fussy of birds. He helps in the feeding, and seems to be a good and careful father. But when the young ones are grown up and able to feed themselves, a curious thing happens. All the gay red-wings in a neighborhood come together in a flock again. And all the young ones and the mothers stay in another flock.

The red-wing is a very nervous and uneasy fellow. While his mate is sitting he is always on guard to see that no harm comes to her. In the picture you can see he looks much concerned, as if he had discovered something. Then he makes a great row if any one comes near. He will give such cries of distress that one would think he was hurt, or that his nestlings were being stolen away. If the enemy is a crow, come to feed quietly on the meadow, he will fly at him, try to peck his head, and annoy him till he goes away. If it is a person who alarms him, he will circle about over his head with loud cries, and now and then swoop down as if he meant to attack him. In fact, he shows so much distress that it is not very pleasant to stay near him.

The young red-wing is just as uneasy and fussy as his papa. As soon as he is able to get out of the nest, he scrambles about in the bushes. He never stays two minutes in one place, and every time his mother comes with food she has to hunt him up before she can give it to him.

The red-wing is fond of green corn, and is often shot by farmers, but he is also a famous insect eater, and earns all the corn he gets. He eats numbers of cut-worms, and other insects, and in some of the prairie States he does great good by eating locusts and their eggs. Besides these, he likes variety, and is fond of the seeds of weeds. Ragweed and smartweed seeds are dainties to him as some nuts are to you, and he eats a great many. So unless a large flock comes to one place to disturb the crops, you may be sure they do more good than harm. So says the Department I told you about.

The young red-winged blackbird is a droll fellow, and has decided notions of his own. Mr. Keyser tells a story of one he picked up. He was put in with some other young birds,—meadowlarks and catbirds. They were all babies together, and all used to being fed. So when the little red-wing got something to eat, they would open their mouths and beg for it, in the pretty bird-baby way. At first he fed them, though he wasn't much more than a baby himself; but they liked it so well that they coaxed everything away from him. He soon got tired of that, and at last refused to feed them at all.

This little bird liked to play jokes on the sober young meadowlarks. His way was to seize one by the wing or tail and dance around the floor, dragging his victim after him. The young larks scolded and held back, and at last they learned to stop his pranks. They did it by throwing themselves over on their backs, and holding up their claws ready to fight.

In spite of this naughty fun, the young blackbird was really fond of them. The larks slept on the ground, and at night, when the little fellows settled down on the floor, the red-wing would often leave his perch and cuddle down by them. This must have been for company only, for it was his way to sleep on a perch.

The Cow-Blackbird, or Cowbird, is another one of this branch of the Blackbird Family who is found all over the United States. He is shining blue-black all over, except his head, which is brown. His mate is entirely brown. He is not quite so large as a red-wing, and he too is a walker.

This bird is called cowbird because he is fond of flying about the cows,—not to trouble them, but to eat the insects that torment them,—which is very pleasant for the cows, I am sure.

There is one queer way that cowbirds have, which no one is able to explain. The cowbird mother does not build a nest for her little family. Yet she wants them well cared for. So she goes slyly about and lays her eggs in other birds' nests. She generally chooses the nest of a smaller bird, though she often uses one belonging to a wood thrush.

Most little birds—warblers and finches—accept the charge. They hatch out the strange egg and bring up the young cowbird, who is bigger than themselves. He is so big that he usually smothers the young ones that belong in the nest. So he receives the whole attention of the little mother bird.

Sometimes other birds come to help one who has a young cowbird to feed, and he grows big and strong. When he is full grown he joins a party of other cowbirds, and they go off in a flock by themselves.

Some small birds will not submit to this. When they find a cowbird's egg in their nest, they go away and leave it there, and make a new nest. Or they make a new story, as I told you the yellow warbler does.

The cowbird has a queer little song. It is something like "cluck-see!" and he seems to squeeze it out as if it were hard work to say it.

FOOTNOTE:

 See Appendix, 15.

XX

THE MEADOW STARLINGS
(*Icteridæ*)—Continued

MEADOWLARK

The meadow starlings are short-tailed birds who live on the ground. They have long bills and mixed sort of plumage, of browns and yellows.

Our common one, called the Meadowlark or Old-Field Lark, though he is not really a lark, is a beautiful bird. He is larger than a robin, and his mottled feathers are set off by a bright yellow breast, with a black crescent under the throat.

This bird lives in the meadows or pastures, and walks about on the ground, where he gets his food. When he wants to sing, he flies up on to a fence, or stands up very straight on a bit of turf, or a stone, and sings away a long time. It is a sweet song, or rather several sweet songs, for he does not always sing the same one.

The mother lark looks like her mate. She makes her nest on the ground, and a snug and cozy home it is. It is none of the open, cup-like nests that anybody can see into. It has a roof, if you please, and sometimes a covered way—like a hall—leading to it. The roof of the nest is made by drawing the grass stems over it and weaving them together. So it is very hard to find. And it is hidden in the long meadow grass besides.

You might think the little family would get hurt when the haymakers came to cut the grass. So they would, if they happened to be there. But lark babies are out of the egg before that time, and they run about as soon as they can stand. Sometimes when a nest has been disturbed, and the birds have had to make a second one, the little ones are not out when the mowers come on. Then there are apt to be sad times in the family. But I have known mowers who carefully cut around a nest, and did not hurt the nestlings. That is a good thing to do, for the birds are so useful and such fine singers that we want as many as we can have.

The meadowlark is a shy bird, and so is more often heard than seen. His song is charming, and he has besides a strange call, a sort of harsh sputter, or chatter, sometimes as he flies over. No doubt he has many more ways of expressing himself, but these are the ones we most often hear.

The Western Meadowlark looks like the Eastern, except that he is a little paler and grayer in color. He has the same general habits, but he is a much finer singer. The song is wilder and has more variety, and sometimes it is very brilliant. It is different in every way from the quiet, rather sad notes that make the Eastern bird so winning.

The Western bird is not so timid as his Eastern brother. He often comes into the towns and sings from the tops of houses. The finest singer I ever heard sang every day from the peak of a low roof. His song to his mate is most charming. It is so low and tender one can hardly hear it.

I once saw a pair of the Western birds nest-making. The little builder was busy filling her beak with dried grasses and such things. For these she had to fly across the road where I sat. Her mate went with her every time. He perched on the fence while she gathered her beakful, watching that no harm came to her. When she went back, he flew across with her and perched on a tree on that side.

All the time he was singing the sweetest low warble, and all the time he was keeping a sharp watch on me. In the West this bird eats beetles, grasshoppers, and the disgusting big black crickets that do so much damage.

XXI

THE ORIOLE BRANCH

(*Icteridæ*)—Continued

It seems odd to put the gay orioles into the Blackbird Family, especially as they don't live on the ground either; but that's where they belong in the books. Orioles live in the trees, and are fine singers. They have sharp-pointed bills, suitable for picking tiny insects out of fruit blossoms. They
have some of the family color,
black, but more orange color, or chestnut red, or yellow. They all make beautiful nests.

The Baltimore oriole is all over the East, the orchard oriole in the South, and the Arizona hooded oriole in the West.

The Baltimore Oriole, who has several other names, such as fire-bird, golden robin, and hang-nest, is a very showy bird, in bright orange and black. He has a fine though short song. His mate is yellow, and brown instead of black, and has a sweet song of her own. Both of them can scold as well as any birds I know.

The nest of this oriole is one of the prettiest we have. It is hung high up in a tall tree, an elm or willow usually, and near the end of a branch, where it swings in the wind. It is a deep bag made of plant fibres, bits of string, and other things. The whole has a gray tint and a silky look, which make it very attractive.

While the mother bird is sitting, her mate stays near and sings a good deal; but when feeding time comes, he works as hard as she in stuffing the hungry little mouths.

As soon as the nestlings are off, they go away in a little party. Then one who looks sharp may often see an oriole papa going quietly about on the ground, with two or three little ones after him, still calling to be fed. He doesn't sing any in these busy days. But sometimes, after the young have learned to feed themselves, he will sing again a little before they all start for their warm winter home in Central America.

It is an anxious time in the bird world when the young are leaving the nest. Orioles are so nervous and make such an outcry over their troubles that we often hear them. The most common accident is the falling of a nestling to the ground. The old birds make so much fuss over it that one would think the baby had fallen into the claws of the cat, at the very least.

They fly around as if they were crazy, shrieking and calling, for they are very fond of their little folk. The youngsters are plucky little fellows. One will hop along till he comes to a tree, and then try to climb the trunk. If he happens to hit on a tree with rough bark, he can do pretty well. He flutters a little way up, and then holds on by the claws till rested. Then he flies a little farther, and so he goes till he reaches a branch.

If it is a smooth trunk he tries, his troubles are great. Sometimes one will scramble up till he comes to a leaf that grows out from the trunk, and hang on to that till he is able to go on. But often one is unable to keep his hold, and falls back into the grass. I have several times picked up a hot and frightened birdling and put him on a branch.

A lady told me an interesting little story, showing how helpful birds are to one another. A Baltimore oriole was picked up from the ground with his wing broken so that he could not fly. The kind-hearted people fixed him comfortably in an attic. They intended to feed him and care for him till he got well and could fly.

They left him there with a window open, so that his wild friends could bring food if they wished. A little while afterward one of them went up to see about the invalid. Behold, he was gone!

They looked for him everywhere, for they knew he could not fly. Suddenly they noticed a great deal of oriole chatter out in the yard. Then they looked carefully over a tree near the window, and there they saw the broken-winged bird in the midst of quite a flock of others.

Of course the outside birds were called by the captive, and they must have carried him out in some way. Birds have been seen to carry off one who was wounded, in two ways. One way was by two birds each taking in his beak a wing of the helpless bird and so flying away with him. This has been seen, and more than once, by men who tell the truth.

The second way birds have been seen to help another was by one getting under the helpless one and so holding him up on the back. This also has been seen by men whose word can be trusted. You remember I told you such a story about the shrike.

So many untrue stories are told about the birds that I am very careful not to tell you anything that is not strictly true.

If you live in the South, you more often see the Orchard Oriole. He is not quite so gay in his dress as the Baltimore. He has chestnut color with his black. His mate is different. She is olive on the back, and yellow below, and she has bright blue legs and feet, which look as if they were covered with kid.

The nest is a hanging one, of course, but it does not usually swing like other oriole nests. It is a little supported at the bottom. It is very beautiful, for it is made of one kind of fine grass. When it is first made, its green color makes it hard to see among the leaves. And as it dries, it turns a rich yellow, like bright clean straw. It is not so high as the Baltimore's, and not hung to the end of a branch. It is often in an apple-tree, for this bird likes to be near people.

The song of the orchard oriole is different from the Baltimore's. It is longer, and has more variety. His mate sings also. Her voice is sweeter than his and not so loud.

If you live in California, the oriole you know will be the Arizona Hooded Oriole. Sometimes he is called the palm-leaf oriole for a reason you will soon see. He is a beautiful, slender bird, having bright orange color with his black. He wears more black than some of the family. His face and throat and tail and wings are of that color, though the wings have two white bars. His mate is yellowish below and olive brown above.

This bird makes the regular oriole family cradle. Sometimes it swings free like the Baltimore's, but not always. It is made of slender, wiry grass, which is green, so that it is hard to see. Sometimes a sort of thread from the edge of palm leaves is used.

This bird sometimes selects a droll place for her nest. She swings it from the under side of a palm or banana leaf. You know a banana leaf is long and wide, and makes a comfortable shade in a hot day; and it does just as well for an umbrella when it rains. It is hard to see how a bird can fasten a nest to a smooth leaf. But Mrs. Grinnell has seen it done in her own yard, and she tells us how the little builder goes to work.

First she takes a thread in her beak and pushes it through the leaf, making a hole, of course. Then she flies around to the other side of the broad leaf, and standing there a minute she pulls the thread through, and pushes it back, making another hole. Thus she goes on, flying from one side to the other till she has sewed her bag to the strong leaf.

Except in the place they choose for their nest, these orioles are about the same as their Eastern cousins, and oriole little folk are the same the world over, I think.

XXII

THE CROW-BLACKBIRD BRANCH

(Icteridæ)—Continued

The fourth branch of this family is of crow-blackbirds and grackles. They have a right to the name of blackbird, for they are quite black. At least they look so a little way off, but if one gets near and sees the sunshine on them, he will see that they reflect blue or green or purple, from their feathers.

Then, too, like others of their family, they go in flocks, and they have a dignified walk on the ground. Some birds who are so social that they like to live in a crowd prefer to go a little apart to nest. But these birds make their rude, clumsy nests all close together.

Blackbirds are fond of corn; who can blame them for that? Thousands of them have been shot because they eat it. But farmers who shoot them forget, or perhaps they do not know, that corn is not the only thing they eat.

Insects as well as birds are fond of corn, and it isn't so easy to keep them away. The birds eat great numbers of them, such as grasshoppers, caterpillars, beetles, and cut-worms, besides mice. All these creatures eat the farmers' crops. So when birds destroy them, they earn some of the corn. They do more than clear the fields of troublesome insects, they eat great quantities of the seeds of weeds that the farmer is always fighting.

Blackbirds are most often seen on the ground, walking around with great dignity. They are looking for food in the grass, or in the field in ploughing time. When they are closely watched, it is often found that they are not in mischief.

Mr. Warren, State Ornithologist of Pennsylvania, tells a story which shows how easy it is to be mistaken. He was with a friend who had thirty acres of corn growing, and was much vexed to see blackbirds walking about among the young plants. They seemed very busy about something, and he was sure they were pulling up his crop. So he got out his guns, and Mr. Warren went with him to punish the birds.

They shot thirty-one of them. Then they began to see what they had been eating. In all the thirty-one, only seven had the least bit of corn, and even they were mostly filled with insects. The rest were stuffed full of insects which do much harm to young corn, mostly cut-worms.

The farmer had killed thirty-one birds who were working for him as hard as they could. No money could hire help that would do so much good as they were doing.

In the Eastern States we have the Crow Blackbird, or Purple Grackle, and the Bronzed Grackle, whose habits are the same.

The purple grackle is a handsome bird, larger than a robin, with very light eyes. His plumage looks black in the shade, but when the sun is on it, shows rich green and blue, and it shines like satin. The bronzed grackle shows purple, and blue, and green, with metallic bronze on the back.

The purple grackle is said to eat corn, and also the eggs and young of other birds. But what he eats has been found out by the Agricultural Department, in the way I told you of. It is given out by them that he does not do so much harm to nests as has been said, and among the crops he does good enough to pay for all the corn he eats.

It is very hard to see just what a bird is eating. It is not even safe to believe all we think we see.

The only time the purple grackle can do more harm than good is when he comes with a big crowd of his friends, and settles down to spend the winter. Then he should be driven away from crops.

I want you to understand me about this. I do not say that these birds never eat the eggs and young of others. What I do say is, that there is plenty of evidence to show that they do it not half so much as people say. I have watched birds for twenty years, as closely, I believe, as any one ever watched them, and I never saw any of the bad deeds that are laid to the blue jay, or the shrike, or the kingbird, or the purple grackle. They may be guilty occasionally, but they are not the villains they are often said to be.

Besides, however bad we may call a few birds, we are ourselves worse. Birds kill only to eat. Many of them are made to feed upon each other, and cannot live in any other way. They kill quickly, and do not generally—if they ever do—torture their prey.

How is it with us? We kill for sport, or for useless show, and we kill in a way that often wounds and leaves our victim to suffer tortures before he dies. Do you think it is fair for us to say hard things about the birds?

In the Rocky Mountains and west of them the common blackbird is Brewer's Blackbird, sometimes called blue-headed grackle. He is not so shy as his brother of the East. He is amiable and friendly with people, and as familiar as the robin in New England. He is often seen in the streets of towns. He will come into yards, and even take food from a doorstep.

Brewer's blackbird is a restless, uneasy fellow, like most of his family. He is always bustling about, and flying hither and thither with rustling wings.

In summer, these birds feed mostly upon insects, which they find on the ground. They have an amusing way of being fair in their feeding. As they walk about in little social parties looking for food, those who come last in the string find the insects nearly all picked up before they get a chance. So they take this clever way of getting their turn at the good things. Every few minutes those in the rear rise and fly over the heads of their friends and alight just before them. So they have the first pick for a while. Then, in a few minutes, those left behind fly over their heads, and take the lead for a time. So, without any quarreling, each one has a fair chance with all the rest. Other birds have found out this way of playing fair. I have seen great blue herons three feet tall do the same thing.

In winter, when insects are scarce, the blackbird turns to grain and the seeds of weeds. But it has been found that he does more good by the weeds he keeps down than harm by the grain he eats.

Brewer's blackbird usually nests in trees, not very high. One time a naturalist going about in Arizona, where are few or no trees, found a curious thing,—a good many blackbird nests, a little settlement one might call it, on the ground, and all strung along close to the edge of a steep bank. At first he could not see why the birds had chosen to be on the edge of a precipice. Then he remembered that horses and cattle roamed over the country, and these animals are careful never to graze close to an edge which might crumble and give them a fall. He concluded that the birds had wit enough to know that. If their nests were out on the plains, they would be likely to be stepped on, but near the edge, they were safe from hoofs.

The common call of Brewer's blackbird is a harsh "chack;" but in the spring he turns musical, and serenades his mate with what we must call songs, because songs are what he intends. They are droll enough to listen to, and not very sweet.

This bird is about the size of a robin, with violet-colored head in the sunlight. His mate is slate-colored.

Birds who live in a crowd learn to be fair in their treatment of one another. An interesting story is told of the way a flock of blackbirds go to bed at night. They come to the roosting-place in little parties from all the country around. One would suppose the first one to get there would choose his place to sleep, and let the last one take what was left.

89

But no! as they arrive, they alight in some big old tree outside the roosting-place. When all are in, they fly up together, circle around for a while, then all settle at the same time in the place where they are to sleep.

XXIII

THE CROW FAMILY
(*Corvidæ*)

This is a large family. Some of our most intelligent birds belong to it. There are first the crows, much larger than a robin and dressed in black. They have long, pointed wings, and tails square at the end. They live in a crowd, and walk on the ground.

Then there are the jays, about the size of a robin, all bright-colored birds. They have short, rounded wings, and long tails which come down almost to a point in the middle.

And then the magpies, between the other two in size. They have tails longer and more pointed than the jays, and are dressed in black with showy white markings.

The common American Crow is a bird that everybody knows. He lives all over our country, and seems to like one part as well as another. There is enough to be said about this bird to fill this whole book. So I shall not try to tell all about him.

The crow is thought by many people to be the most knowing bird in America, and he is the one who has been most abused. He does some mischief, it is true, but he does a great deal more good. So say the officers of the Department who have looked into his food. They have found that he does pull up some corn; but he stuffs himself and his family with thousands, and even millions, of grubs, and insects, and mice, and other small creatures, that would have done far more damage to the crops than he.

Farmers have often killed or driven away the crows, because they thought they were hurting their crops. But sometimes they have found out their mistake, and have been glad to get them back again.

A story comes from the West which shows what I mean. One year the farmers were alarmed to see a great many crows around their fields. They had never seen so many there. Of course they thought they had come to eat the corn, so they began to kill them. I won't tell you the ugly story of the war against the birds. After it had gone on awhile, the farmers began to notice that crows were not the only ones who had come. A new grub that they had never seen before was on hand. There were millions of them, and they were always hungry. Young corn plants seemed to suit them, and when corn was gone, they began eating the grass.

It never came into the farmers' heads that the birds had anything to do with the grubs. So they kept up their war on the crows till few were left.

It's easier to drive away birds than insects, so the grubs went on eating. There were no crows left to trouble, and yet the crops got smaller every year. At last some one had sense enough to see that the crows had come on purpose to eat the grubs, and that they had driven away their best friends, the most useful helpers they could possibly have.

When they saw how stupid they had been, they began to coax the birds back. They sent out and had crows caught and brought to their fields to work for them. The birds took hold of the business, and made short work of the corn-eating grub, and the farmers learned a good lesson.

You may think it strange that the crows should know where the grubs were, but birds are very sharp to find their food. It is well known that when there gets to be an unusual number of insects in one place, more birds will come to feed on them. Some time when you are in the country when grass is cut, notice how many birds will come to eat the grasshoppers and other creatures that are uncovered when the hay is taken away.

The crows take the same fair way of going to roost that the Brewer's blackbirds do.

I could tell you stories—true ones, too—all day about this bird, and his services to the farmer. We all know how wise he is, and how hard it is to trap him.

I will give you one little story, to show his kindness to his fellows. Then, when you have a chance to watch one, I hope you will take pains to see for yourself what he does and what he eats. Do not believe all you hear or read about him, for I'm sorry to say there are some persons who like so well to tell a sensational story that they do not take any trouble to find out if it is true.

The story is this. Two crows were caught and kept in a large cage out of doors. It happened to be a time when food for birds was rather scarce. Some one noticed that the birds seemed to eat a good deal, and he set himself to watch them. He found that the prisoners in the cage were giving some of their food through the bars to their hungry friends outside. Could men be more unselfish?

There is no end to the funny pranks that are told of crows who have been tamed and lived with people. One that I heard of liked to get out in the yard when clothes from the wash were hung out. He would walk along on the clothesline and pull out every clothespin, carrying each one to the roof and laying it safely away. Of course this let the wet garments fall in the dirt, and he was scolded well for his mischief. Then he would fly up to the roof and throw every pin down to the ground, as if he said, "Well, take your old clothespins!"

Another tame crow was very fond of pulling over a work-basket, and scattering the spools and thimbles and other things in it. One day he got hold of a paper of needles. This he opened, and then went on to hide them, which crows always like to do with everything. He took each needle and pushed it into the bed, as if it were a cushion, and hammered each one in out of sight.

I hope you know the Blue Jay. He is a beautiful bird in different shades of blue, set off with white and black, and with a fine crest. His mate is the same. This is the jay we know in the East and South.

BLUE JAY

He is a noisy bird, full of fun and antics. He makes himself heard wherever he goes. This has given him the name of being quarrelsome. It is often said that he is always fighting. But that is a mistake, made because people do not look closely enough. He is boisterous and jolly, but he rarely quarrels.

There is one time in his life when he is as still as a mouse. Then he comes to his tree so quietly that you cannot hear him. That is when there is a nest to look after.

The nest of a blue jay is usually not very high, in a tree. While his mate is sitting, he takes the best care of her. He brings food to her, and often sings to her. This song is very low; one can hardly hear it; but it is one of the sweetest of bird songs.

No bird is more loving to his little folk than the blue jay, and not one is more frantic when anything happens to them. James Russell Lowell, the poet, loved the birds, and has written delightful things about them. He once found a family of young blue jays who seemed to be in trouble. He had a ladder brought, and went up to the nest to see if he could help them. He found that they had got caught in the nest lining, and could not get away. They were full grown, and the old birds had worked hard from morning till night to keep them fed.

As soon as Mr. Lowell saw what was the matter, he took out his knife to cut the strings that held them. At first when he came near, the old birds were very much frightened. They flew around his head and cried, and were going to fight him. But jays are wise birds, and in a moment they saw that he did not mean to hurt them. So they perched close by him, so near he could put his hand on them. Then they watched him while he cut the little ones loose. All of them could fly, and they did, at once.

One of the nestlings had been so tightly held that one leg was withered and dead, but the next day Mr. Lowell saw him hopping about the garden path, on one leg, while his parents brought him food, and took great care of him.

91

The blue jay, like most birds, is kind to others. One man found a little flock taking care of an old, blind jay. They fed him, and led him to water to bathe. They warned him of danger, and in every way looked out for his comfort as if he were a nestling.

Besides being a singer, this bird is a mimic. He can imitate the songs of other birds, as well as many other sounds. A lady once had a blue jay who had fallen from the nest. She brought him up, and he was very tame. She told me that he learned to sing like a mockingbird, and did it almost as well. This bird was very fond of her. When she tried to give him his freedom, he wouldn't have it. If she slipped away from him, he would sit up in a tree and scream like a lost child. Then, when she came into his sight, he would fly down to her shoulder and rub his head against her cheek like a kitten, he was so happy to be back with her.

The blue jay is a useful bird. Dr. Brewer says that one pair of jays will feed their young in one season five hundred thousand caterpillars; also that one pair of jays will destroy one million insect eggs in a winter.

Many hard things have been said about this bird,—for one thing, that he eats eggs and young birds. You will notice, however, that many who repeat these stories about him say, "I have not seen the bird do so, but some one else has." Testimony like this is worth nothing. Such things are copied from one book to another because it is much easier to take what is set down in the books than to go out and see for one's self. Often a story which has no truth in it is said over and over till people believe it because they have heard it so often.

Believe me, the blue jay is not half so bad as he is painted, and he has many lovable traits to make up for what he does do.

Mr. Keyser brought up a young blue jay from the nest. He put him for a while into a cage with two young orioles. Like all young birds, all three of the youngsters were hungry, and expected everybody to feed them. So the young jay opened wide his mouth, and waited for something good to drop into it. He was met by the two orioles with their mouths wide open. There they stood, face to face, all asking to be fed. It was a funny sight.

Then the blue jay baby was put into another cage, where were two young catbirds. To these he was very loving. He would sidle up to them and caress them, stroking their backs and wings with his bill. He insisted on sleeping between the two on the perch. He looked very droll with a small bird on each side of him, all snuggled up together.

After a while the blue jay had a whole cage to himself. Then the other cages were moved to the front porch, and he was left alone on the back porch. This did not please him at all; he was lonely. He called and cried and fretted about till he was placed beside the others. Then he gave a cry of joy, and really squealed with delight.

The West is richer than the East in jays. There are several in the Rocky Mountains and California. Steller's Jay is said to represent the Eastern bird I have been telling about. He is different in looks and larger. He is darker blue, with some sooty brown, and he has a fine crest. But he is the same noisy, jolly fellow as his cousin on the Atlantic side of the country.

If your home is in the West, beyond the Mississippi River, of course you know the American Magpie. He is a large, splendid fellow, who looks especially fine when he is flying over your head.

AMERICAN MAGPIE

The magpie is all in black and white: white below and in shoulder patches, and black on the breast and above. In the sunlight he shows purple and blue and green shades over the black. He has a very long tail, which is wide in the middle and runs down almost to a point at the end. This is very showy, when he spreads it wide in flying.

In California the magpie shows a curious variation. On one side of the mountains the magpie has a yellow bill, but the magpie on the other side has a black one, though in every other way they seem to be the same.

The magpie is a social bird. Even in nesting time he likes plenty of neighbors. A party of them will settle in a little grove and build several nests in it. The nests of this bird are the queerest bird homes you ever saw. They look like big covered baskets. They are half the size of a bushel basket, and made of sticks outside. There is an opening on each side for the bird to go in and out. Those I have seen were in the tops of low trees.

The beautiful tail of the magpie seems to be a great care to him. When he flies,—as I said,—he spreads it wide and makes a great show with it. When he is going about on a tree, he jerks and twitches it all the time. No doubt every jerk means something, if we could only understand. When on the ground, he holds the precious tail up carefully, so that it shall not touch the earth. He is a very dignified bird when walking about in this way, looking for the grubs, grasshoppers, crickets, and other creatures on which he feeds. But sometimes he has no dignity at all. He scolds, and screams, and acts like a bad child. He isn't particular about his food. He will eat almost anything, even scraps from a kitchen.

Major Bendire tells a comical story of the cunning of some magpies in getting food away from a dog. The dog carried his bone with some meat on it to the lawn in front of the major's tent, and lay down to enjoy it, dog-fashion. In a minute or two, a little party of six magpies came around, probably hoping to be invited to dinner. The dog did not take the hint, but went on gnawing.

93

Then the birds seemed to consider, and after a few minutes they placed themselves around the dog. One stood right in front of his nose about two feet away. Another one took his place close to the dog's tail, while two stood on each side.

When all the birds were ready, the one by the tail gave it a sharp peck. No dog could stand that insult. The victim forgot his bone, wheeled around, and dashed after that bird. He did not catch him with the first grab, and the wily bird fluttered away. He did not go fast enough to show the dog he could not catch him, but he led him on and kept him eager to get at him as long as he could.

But what happened to the dog's dinner all this time? Of course you have guessed that the instant the dog left, the five hungry magpies pounced upon the bone. They didn't mind eating at the second table. They knew their time was short, and they made good use of it. I'm afraid they "gobbled."

When the dog saw that he couldn't catch the magpie, he thought of his dinner, and came back. The birds stepped one side, and he took his place again.

Of course the birds were not half satisfied, and besides, one of them had not had even a taste. So they made ready to play the little trick again. Now see their fair play with one another! The bird who had coaxed the dog away had his turn at the head of the table, while another one did the teasing. They repeated this several times, and each time a different bird led the dog away.

The major was a trained observer, and he could tell the birds apart. One had a longer tail, another had a broken feather, and another was smaller. So he could easily see that each time a different bird had the best chance. He was sure they had planned the whole thing out.

I once had a chance to study the ways of some magpies. The birds were busy in their nests, and I was well hidden and quiet, so they did not see me. I heard much soft, gentle talk from them, and at last a sweet song. I was much surprised at this, and hoped to know a good deal more about them, but the next time I called on them, they saw me. Such a row as they made! They flew around my head, shouting and screaming at me, till I was glad to get out of the grove. I could not blame the birds, for magpies are much prized as cage-birds. They readily learn to talk, and are intelligent and interesting pets, so that the nests are robbed all the time. Of course they are ready to fight for their little ones.

FOOTNOTE:

See Appendix, 16.

XXIV

THE LARK FAMILY

(*Alaudidæ*)

There are a good many kinds of larks in the world, but only one comes to us, the Horned Lark, or shore lark. He differs a little in color in the various places he is found over our broad country, but not enough to call him another species.

In places where there is a great deal of rain, birds take on a slightly different shade from their brothers who live in dry places. So there are several varieties of the horned lark. But dress isn't everything, and, after all, he is the same bird in habits and manners wherever we find him in the United States. He is streaked brown on the back, and white below, with yellow throat and black and white markings.

The way you may always know a Prairie Horned Lark, of whom I will speak, is by the pretty little tufts of feathers that stand up on his head like horns, and the very long nail on his hind toe.

DESERT HORNED LARK

Another way you may know this bird is that he lives on the ground, and never perches in a tree. Sometimes he gets up on a fence to sing, but he likes best to run along the road, or in a field, and he never—never hops. The place to look for him is a field or pasture, or on a country road.

When insects are abroad, he eats the more dainty small ones, young grasshoppers and locusts before they get big and tough, small beetles and larvæ; and baby larks are fed on them. But he doesn't starve when they are gone; he is fond of seeds of weeds and grasses.

The nest of the horned lark is on the ground, and the little mother is very clever in hiding it, and not showing people where it is. Many birds, you know, will stay on the nest till one almost steps on them, and then fly up with a great fuss, thus telling their secret. When the wise little lark sees one coming, she quietly slips off her nest. Then she crouches to the ground, and creeps away. When she thinks she is far enough, she rises to her full height, and begins to eat, or to walk around as if she had nothing on her mind, and there were no such thing as a nest anywhere about. No matter how long one may stay there hoping to find the nest, she will not go back, not even to see if it is safe, so long as any one is near. If all birds were so wily, there would be fewer nests robbed, and we should have more birds.

The little home so carefully guarded is well made. The bird scratches out a little hollow and lines it with grass or thistledown, that is, if she can't get what she likes best. Her choice is for nice soft mullein leaves, which she pulls to pieces. These, you know, are thick and smooth, and must make a warm, dry bed for the little larks.

The brave little mother nests so early that she is often caught in a snowstorm. Nests have been found with the bird on them, when the snow had to be brushed away to get at her, actually sitting under the snow.

When the young larks can run about, and before they can fly, the father takes them in charge. Then the mother sits again, and hatches out another brood.

The horned lark sings on the wing, as does the skylark of Europe that we've heard so much about. It is supposed that he cannot equal that famous bird, but so few have heard him, it is hardly safe to say so. I once heard a horned lark sing. He ran across the road in front of the carriage, flew to a fence, and gave an exquisite little song. If it had come down to us while the singer was soaring about over our heads, I think few bird songs could have excelled it.

The feather tufts which are called horns stand up when the bird is excited. Usually they lie back nearly flat on the head.

In the picture you can see one of these birds in his usual attitude, walking.

95

FOOTNOTE:

_ See <u>Appendix, 17</u>.

XXV

THE FLYCATCHING FAMILY

(*Tyrannidæ*)

Larks may be scarce, but we have plenty of flycatchers, and they all look very much alike. They are mostly in dull colors, and they have a way of raising the head feathers which gives them a little crest. Then they have rather thick necks, and they sit up very straight on the perch.

They catch living flies, as you see by the name, and they have their own way of doing it. No flycatcher ever scrambles around like a fussy little warbler, snatching a fly here and there. Far from it! It is a dignified family, and none of them ever seems to be in a hurry.

The true flycatcher way to get a dinner is to sit still and wait. The very babies in the nest are patient little fellows. They never make half the row over their dinner that young robins do. They could give lessons in table manners to some young folks I have seen. And waiting seems to be a good way, for nobody is better fed than a flycatcher.

KINGBIRD

On his perch the waiting bird sits perfectly still, but keeps a sharp lookout all around him. When a fly or other insect comes near that he thinks he will like, he dashes out and catches it as it flies. Then he goes back to his perch and waits for another.

Some of the family have the habit of singing as they wait. The wood pewee drawls out his sweet "pee-u-ee," the phœbe sings his sharp "phœ-be" by the hour, and the least flycatcher snaps out his "chebec" till we are tired of hearing him.

Flycatchers are classed among birds who do not sing, but several of them do sing,—not loud, like a robin, but low, quiet songs to the mate or the nestlings.

One of the best known of the flycatchers all over the country is the Kingbird. He is a little smaller than a robin, and all in brownish black, with white breast. He has also white tips to his tail feathers, which look very fine when he spreads it out wide in flying.

Among the head feathers of the kingbird is a small spot of orange color. This is called in the books a "concealed patch" because it is seldom seen, it is so hidden by the dark feathers.

This bird does much good by eating many insects. It is often said that he eats bees. But a curious thing has been found out about this habit. It seems he has a choice in bees. He is fond of the drones which make no honey, and so are not useful in a hive. He will hunt drones all day, but he is shy of a honey bee. Do you know why? The bird has not told us, but we can guess that it is because the honey bee is armed with a sting, and can make it very uncomfortable for any bird who catches her.

There is another reason too why the bird may prefer the drone. The honey bee usually flies low, where the flowers are, while the drone isn't after flowers and flies higher in the air. The kingbird sits higher than the honey bee flies, and the drones are the ones that come near him.

Another insect that the kingbird is fond of is the robber fly, which destroys hundreds of honey bees. That should make every bee-keeper his friend.

These things have been found out in the way I told you, by shooting the birds to see what they had been eating.

Mr. Bryant, who knows birds well, tells of a bee-keeper in California who saw a great many kingbirds among his bees. Of course he thought they were eating them, and he killed one hundred of them. On looking into their stomachs to see if they had eaten honey bees, he found them filled with drones. They had been working for him all the time, for every bee-keeper likes to have drones killed.

It has been said that the kingbird is annoying to other birds, and he is called a tyrant. I wanted to know if this was true. I did not go to books to find out, for many people—as I have told you—do not study for themselves, but repeat what some one else has said. The way I took to find out was to notice the ways of every kingbird I could see. For many years I have watched them hours at a time, for weeks together. I spend every summer among the birds, and almost everywhere I go I find kingbirds.

In this way I have found out that the kingbird is one of the most peaceable of birds. He drives strangers away from the tree where his nest is, and so does every other bird. The crow he seems to consider his enemy, and often flies after him, but excepting that, I have never seen a kingbird disturb any bird who was minding his own business. He is not half so much of a tyrant as the robin or the hummingbird.

The kingbird is quiet and devoted to his family. He seems never to tire of catching insects. While young ones are in the nest, he may usually be seen from morning till night, sitting very straight upon a low perch, looking for flies of many kinds.

Let me tell you a little story of a kingbird which I can assure you is true, for a gentleman whose word may be relied upon saw it near enough to be perfectly sure of the facts.

A big bird, he did not notice what kind, was flying off with a nestling robin in his claws. All at once a kingbird flew at him so fiercely that he had to drop the young one to defend himself. The youngster could not fly, and of course began to fall. When the kingbird saw that, he left the thief and flew under the little bird. He held it up on his back, and flew carefully to the ground, where it slipped off safely.

When a kingbird has been tamed and kept in a house, he has been found to be a very knowing fellow. One that I heard of saw that the people were friendly, and he lost all fear of them. His greatest pleasure seemed to be to keep warm. He would cuddle up to a lighted lamp, and dearly liked to crawl under the bedclothes. This pet was quiet and dignified, never a chatterbox. The only sounds he made were a few low notes like thanks, when he was fed.

The nest of the kingbird is usually placed in a low tree like the apple-tree. It is made of anything that comes handy. I have seen one of white wool where sheep were kept, and one of gray moss on the seashore where it is found in plenty.

The Western kingbird differs in color from the Eastern. He is more gray, with under parts bright yellow. He is said to be more social and more noisy than the sober Eastern bird. But in other respects they are much alike.

This bird has been called quarrelsome, but persons who look closely at birds have said that what careless observers have called quarrels are really play. For the Western kingbird, the Arkansas Kingbird of the books, is a rather jolly fellow, says Major Bendire.

All flycatchers are useful and should be carefully protected, says the same well-informed writer.

The Wood Pewee is another common flycatcher. He is not generally seen about houses like the phœbe, who calls from the peak of the barn. He may be found in the orchard or the edge of the woods. There he will stand on a fence or low branch and sing or call by the hour, every few minutes flying out to catch a passing insect.

This bird is in dark colors, with whitish breast and two white wing-bars. His common call is a plaintive, long-drawn-out "pee-u-ee" and sometimes "pee-ay," but he can sing a droll little song. One lady who watched a wood pewee build her nest heard her sing to herself as she worked what sounded like "O-wee-wee-wee."

The nest made by this little mother is very pretty. It is most often on a dead limb where a branch starts out, making a broad foundation. For this reason the bird is called in the South, the dead-limb bird. The nests are not all alike. I have seen many closely covered with lichen, and some made of gray moss so thin that the eggs could be seen through it. Whatever it is made of, it is low and flat like a saucer, and so much like the branch it is on that it is not easy to see.

Like other bird mothers, the wood pewee is devoted to her nestlings. She will shield them from the rain by sitting close on the nest and making an umbrella of herself. And when the sun comes down very hot on them, she has been seen to perch on the edge of the nest and spread her wings to act as a shade for them. It is pretty to see this bird with her little family when they have left the nest and are being taught to take care of themselves. She makes many sweet little noises which sound like talk, or a sort of whispering.

The Western Wood Pewee looks like his Eastern brother, but he is a very different bird. His dress is about the same, and he catches his flies in pewee fashion, but his voice is not in the least like that we hear on the Atlantic side of the country.

The Eastern wood pewee has a low, sweet voice, of which one cannot get tired. But the bird of the West has loud, harsh notes, so dismal in tone that they are painful to listen to. His song is almost the only really unpleasant bird song I know.

The nest of this bird is a rather deep cup saddled on to a large limb. When it is in a cottonwood grove, it is covered with the sticky white cotton from the trees. It is very pretty when fresh, but it soon gets soiled, and then it is not nice to look at or to handle.

FOOTNOTE:

 See Appendix, 18.

XXVI

THE HUMMING FAMILY

(*Trochilidæ*)

This is an American family, and no country in the world can show a more beautiful one. There are more than four hundred species, and some of them hardly bigger than a bee. All of these birds have brilliant colors that are called metallic. That is, they glitter like metal, and they show different colors when they are turned different ways.

All hummingbirds fly very swiftly. You know how they go,—not straight like most birds, but darting one way and another so quickly they can hardly be seen. As they fly, their wings move so fast they look almost like little clouds, and we hear the low noise we call humming.

Hummingbirds eat nothing but tiny insects, and the honey of flowers, which they suck up through their long bill. They take their food without alighting, for they can hold themselves still before a flower, with the wonderful wings, as long as they choose.

The bill of a hummingbird is much longer than his head. It is something like a pair of tubes through which he can draw up the sweet juices he likes. The tongue is long too, and it can be pushed out far beyond the end of the bill. It looks like a stiff white thread.

We have in the Eastern States but one species, the ruby-throat, but there are several in California.

No bird is more charming than our common Ruby-throated Hummingbird. He is most often seen flitting about among the flowers. But now and then one may catch him sitting demurely on a dead twig, dressing his tiny feathers.

This bird is all in green, with a brilliant ruby-colored throat, which looks like a gem as he darts about. His mate is in green also, but her throat is white.

You would not think this pretty midget could be a fighter, but he is. When a hummingbird finds a vine full of sweet blossoms, or a bed of bright nasturtiums, or any good place to feed in, he claims the whole of it for himself. He tries to drive away every other hummingbird who comes near it. Sometimes two of them will carry on a quarrel over a honeysuckle vine for days.

The hummingbird is the most pugnacious bird in America. If he were as big as a crow, he would be a terror to man and beast, for he is afraid of nothing. This spirited mite of a bird will even attack an eagle, who is big enough to eat him at a mouthful. He beats him too, for he comes down on top of his head, where the big, clumsy fellow cannot get at him. There he pecks and pulls out feathers till the eagle is glad to get out of his clutches.

A hummingbird's nest is one of the prettiest things in the world. It is not much bigger than a walnut, and is made of soft plant down, usually of a yellowish gray color.

Perhaps you don't see how plant down can be made to keep in shape, without twigs or grasses to hold it. If you could see the bird make it, you would understand at once. She brings her stuff in small mouthfuls, and works it into a solid mass by strong efforts with beak and feet. She pokes and prods each tiny bunch as she brings it, till she makes it all hold together. It is a sort of felt.

Then the little worker covers the outside with bits of lichen picked off the trees, and held on, it is said, by cobwebs. This makes the nest look exactly like the branch it is on. So it is very hard to see.

It takes a hummingbird several days of hard work to make a nest, because she can bring only a little at a time. She does it alone too; her mate has not been seen to help her at all.

I think the male ruby-throat does not help in the nest-building because the little mother will not let him. She knows just how the cradle is to be made, and she doesn't want him to bother her. She likes to have her nest to herself just as she likes to have her honeysuckle to herself. I don't say positively that is the reason, you know; I only guess it is.

After the nest is made, and two eggs about as big as small beans are laid, the hummingbird begins to sit. When the nestlings come out of the egg, they are about the size of honey bees, with bills no larger than the head of a common pin. Twenty-one days they stay in the nest and are fed by their hard-working little mother.

When the twins get their feathers, and their bills are growing longer and longer, they sit up across the top of the nest, side by side. Then they are very pretty, and not at all afraid of people. They will let one gently stroke their backs. They will even answer in a soft murmur one who talks to them.

Hummingbirds are never so afraid of people as other birds. They are easily tamed. But they should never be caged, for they will not live long in a house. They need food that we cannot give them.

A man had a hummingbird whom he kept alive a long time by letting him go free when he seemed to need change of food. He would fly off, but always came back. After the bird got to be very tame, the man brought two young hummingbirds and put them in the cage with him. He did not notice them much till they began to droop. Then the man opened the door to let them out.

At once the elder bird took the little ones in charge, and coaxed them to fly out with him. He led them to a place where he had found the tiny spiders these birds like, and showed them how to get what they wanted. They all ate their fill and then came back to the house, where they were well contented to be.

The way the mother hummingbird feeds her babies is curious. When she comes with food, she alights on the edge of the nest, and pulls a little one up so that she can get at it. Then she runs her long, slim bill down its throat, and pokes the food in with little jerks. It looks as if it would kill the youngster, but he seems to like it. Anyway, he grows very fast, and—as I said—in three weeks he is beautifully feathered, with a bill as long as his mother's, and ready to fly.

A lady who had two young hummingbirds told me that they slept so soundly they were like dead birds. One could take them up and carry them about, and they would not wake. In cold weather she often wrapped one up in a piece of flannel and laid him in a soft, warm place, and he never stirred till morning.

The way she got this pair of birds was interesting. She was walking in the woods and broke a dead branch from a tree, to use for something. On turning it over she saw a nest, and strange to say two little birds in it. She had been holding it upside down, but they had held on so tightly that they did not fall out.

The lady did not know what to do. She did not want baby hummingbirds, but she couldn't put the branch back, and she was afraid their mother would not find them if she left them. So she took them home. She had no trouble to feed them, and they lived with her six weeks, and died by accident at last.

It is thought that the male ruby-throat does not come to the nest at all, but he must have some way of knowing how things are going on. At Mrs. Wright's summer home a mother hummingbird was killed in a hailstorm, while young were in the nest. At once the father, or at least a male bird, came and fed and took care of the nestlings till they flew.

In California one of the most common of this family is Anna's Hummingbird. He is green, with a throat and crown of changeable colors, lilac and red.

The nest of this bird is usually, like the ruby-throat's, of plant down covered with lichens. But some have been found made of the blossoms of the eucalyptus, or gum-tree. This bird is as easily tamed as the ruby-throat, and seems to act a good deal like him.

Mrs. Grinnell found a nest in her yard in California. The mother allowed herself to be photographed in many positions. The young ones were never afraid, and did not mind the camera in the least. Hummingbirds never seem to have any fear of people.

FOOTNOTE:

See Appendix, 19.

XXVII

THE SWIFT FAMILY

(*Micropodidæ*)

Swifts are curious birds, with strange habits. The one we know by sight in the East is the chimney swift. Most like him in the West is Vaux's swift. His ways are like the common chimney swift's, and his looks nearly the same.

The Chimney Swift is often called the chimney swallow, but it is very easy to tell one from a swallow. One way is, that when a swift is flying about over our heads, he looks as if he had no tail. The tail is very short, not half so long as the wing. He looks more like a bat than a bird.

Then the swift flies in a different way. A swallow soars a good deal, that is, moves without beating the wings, a sort of gliding through the air. But a swift beats the wings much more frequently. A swallow will often alight on a telegraph-wire or a roof. A swift is said never to alight except to sleep.

This bird is so much at home on wing that he even gets the twigs to make the nest while flying. These twigs are the smallest ones on the ends of dead branches, and are easily snapped off. The bird flies at them, snatches one in beak or feet, breaks it off, and goes right on, without stopping.

When he gets his twig, he carries it to a dark, sooty chimney. A queer place for a home, surely. They used to choose a hollow tree or a cave to live in, and that seems much nicer. But chimneys are now more plentiful than hollow trees. And besides, they are nearer the bird's food. So chimney homes are now the fashion in the swift family.

To make a swift nest, the twigs are glued to the chimney in the shape of a little bracket. The glue is the saliva of the bird, which is gummy, and gets hard as it dries, and looks like isinglass.

The mouth of a chimney swift is very odd. You have heard of "stretching a mouth from ear to ear." That's just what the swift does every time he opens his. It needs to be big, for he gathers up his food in it. While he is flying around in the air, he is busy catching tiny flying creatures, such as flies and beetles, and thus keeping the air clear for us.

The tail of this bird is another queer thing. It has no soft feathery tips like most birds' tails. It ends in sharp spines, like needles. These are most useful to brace him against the rough chimney where he sleeps. These spines are really the stiff shafts or stems of the feathers, sticking out beyond the plumey part.

The chimney swift hangs himself up to sleep. He fastens his sharp claws into the rough bricks, and props himself firmly with his spiny tail. Even when the young swift is but two weeks old, he crawls out of the nest and hangs himself up under it. He seems to like that for a change from forever lying in a narrow bracket.

Chimney swifts are social birds. They can't bear to be alone. They are almost always seen flying about in small parties, and calling to each other as they go, a strange, chattering cry. They are of a sooty color suitable to their sooty home, and the pair are alike. Vaux's swift is a little smaller and paler than the common chimney swift.

The young swift is longer in his nursery than any bird of his size in the United States. He is four weeks old before he ventures out of his grimy home, though before that he will come up to the door to be fed.

A late writer in a newspaper tells a little story showing the affection of a chimney swift for her little one. The writer had watched all summer a party of swifts who lived in one of his chimneys. A month or more after he supposed that all had flown away to the South beyond our southern boundary, where they spend the winter, he heard the twittering of one in the chimney. He took out the fireboard and found there a young bird. He was full grown and able to fly, but he was fastened by a horsehair to the nest. This had been pulled off by his weight, and lay on the hearth, holding him prisoner.

The little fellow seemed to know he was to be helped, for he lay still while the man looked to see what was the matter. His mother soon came into the chimney with food. She took her place beside the man and waited, while he cut the strong hair and set the nestling free.

Then the old bird went to work to teach him to fly. It was an hour or more before he learned to use his wings. As soon as he did, the two started off on their lonely journey to the far South, to join their friends who had been gone so long. How I wish we could know that they reached them.

Insects were about gone when this happened, and this swift mother would have died if she had stayed, but she would not leave her little one to starve.

It is a beautiful thing to see a large flock of swifts go to bed. If they all rushed in pell-mell, they might hurt one another. They begin by flying around high above the chimney in great circles. As they go around they sink lower, and the circles get smaller till it looks like an immense whirling funnel. When the birds forming the lower part of the funnel reach the top of the chimney, they plunge in. So in a short time the whole flock is in and no one hurt.

FOOTNOTE:

_ See Appendix, 20.

XXVIII

THE GOATSUCKER FAMILY

(*Caprimulgidæ*)

These are queer-looking birds, having their front toes tied together by a kind of webbing, and almost no hind toe at all. The mouth, too, is almost as odd as the toes. It has a short beak, but is very wide, and it opens from ear to ear like the swift's. The plumage is so soft that the birds can fly without making the least sound.

The two most common goatsuckers are the whip-poor-will and the nighthawk. They are both as large as a robin, and stouter. They are dressed in dull brown, and black and white, mottled all over. If you just glanced at the two, you might think them alike. But they are not marked alike, and all their ways are so different that there is no trouble in telling them apart.

The Whip-poor-will has broad white tailmarks, with stripes on the back, and a narrow white band across the breast. He comes out only in the evening, and he flies low, without making a sound. He rests lengthwise of a log or fence, not across it as most birds do. His feet are too short to clasp a perch.

On his log or fence the whip-poor-will sits and sings while he waits for his supper. You all know his song, his lively "whip-poor-will" over and over many times. It is a delightful evening sound, which I love to hear. It is said that his notes have been counted, and he has been found to repeat them several hundred times without stopping.

When moths or other creatures which fly in the night come along, he catches them in his big mouth. But he is not obliged always to wait. Sometimes he flies near the ground like a shadow, looking for prey, and he often hops awkwardly along the road, for the same purpose. He picks up straggling insects, and in the West locusts.

The whip-poor-will mother makes no nest. She finds a little hollow in the ground, among leaves or near bushes in the woods, and that's good enough for her nestlings. She lays two eggs, speckled and mottled so that they look like the ground and leaves around them. She looks almost the same herself. You might walk close to her and not see her.

When young whip-poor-wills come out of the egg, they are dressed in speckled gray down. They cuddle down quietly by their mother, and the whole family is hard to see. When their eyes are shut, they look almost exactly like the earth and leaves among which they lie.

If a whip-poor-will nest is disturbed, the mother will pretend to be badly hurt. She will tumble about on the ground and cry like the whine of a young puppy, trying to coax away the one she fears. If she is too much alarmed, she will clasp her young one between her feet and fly away with it.

Instead of the common whip-poor-will of the Northern and Middle States, the South has the Chuck-will's-widow, who is somewhat larger. The West has the Poor-will, or the Nuttall's Whip-poor-will, who is rather smaller and paler than either. The habits of all are about the same. They are called solitary birds. That is, they are not found in parties like swallows or crows. They do not sing or call when flying.

These birds are hard to watch because they come out in the dark, and can then see so much better than we can. So we know little about their ways.

The Nighthawk's looks, and all his ways, are different. He wears the same colors that the whip-poor-will does, but they are arranged in another way. They are put in bars running across the back and tail, and there is a great deal of white on his upper breast. On the wing is a large white spot that looks like a hole across it, when you see him flying away up in the air. You can always know him by this.

NIGHTHAWK

Then he does not act like the whip-poor-will. He is a high flyer, sailing about over our heads in the afternoon or evening. He is not silent on the wing. Now and then he gives a strange sharp cry like "peent." He is busy catching flies and mosquitoes as he goes. Sometimes you will see him dive head first toward the earth as if he would dash himself against it. At the same time he makes a loud sound, like blowing into the bunghole of an empty barrel. But before he touches, he turns and skims along just above the ground.

The mother nighthawk, like the whip-poor-will, makes no nest. She chooses a sunny spot in a pasture or on a hillside to put her eggs. Sometimes in the cities, where flies and other things to eat are so plentiful, she takes a flat house-roof for her nursery. Many pairs of down-covered baby night hawks are brought up over our heads, and we do not know it.

The family name of Goatsuckers was given to the birds from the foolish notion that they took milk from the goats. By watching them, it has been found that when they are so busy around the goats or cattle, they are really catching the insects which torment them. So they are doing a kindness to the beasts, instead of an injury.

FOOTNOTE:

See Appendix, 21.

XXIX

THE WOODPECKER FAMILY

(Picidæ)

You may generally know a woodpecker the moment you see him on a tree. He will—if he follows woodpecker fashions—be clinging to the trunk, or a big branch, propped up by his stiff tail, and not perched crosswise like most other birds.

There are a good many of this family in the world. We have twenty-four species in North America. They differ from other birds in two or three ways. First their toes are always in pairs, two turned forward and two turned backward, except in one genus, which has but three toes. So they can hold on better than anybody else.

Then again the tails of woodpeckers are not like most birds' tails. They are strong and stiff, so that they can be used as props to hold the bird in the queer position he likes so well.

Oddest of all are the woodpecker tongues. They are round, worm-shaped it is called, and except in the genus of sapsuckers, very long. They can be pushed out far beyond the end of the beak. That is so that they can reach into a deep hole for the insects they eat. They have little barbs or sharp points on the tip, to catch their prey, and they are sticky besides. The tongue of the sapsucker has a brush at the end and is not barbed.

One of the most notable things about a woodpecker is his bill, which he uses as a drill and also to drum with.

Woodpeckers are made to take care of the large limbs and trunks of trees, to get out from under the bark the grubs which would kill them. They are perfectly fitted for the work.

As you learn more about birds and beasts, you will see that every one is exactly fitted for his work in life. A worm is as well fitted to be a worm as a bird is to be a bird. How this came to be so has long been a study of the wise men, and they have not found out all about it yet.

The largest of this family that is common is the Golden-winged Woodpecker, or Flicker. He is as large as a pigeon. In the Eastern States is the golden-wing, in the West and California the red-shafted, who differs merely in the dress.

The gold-winged woodpecker has a brown back with black bars, and a light breast with heavy black spots. His wings and tail are yellow on the inside. He has a bright red collar on the back of his neck, a heavy black crescent on his breast, and black cheek patches or bars running down from the corners of his mouth.

The Red-shafted Flicker has red cheek patches instead of black, and omits the red collar altogether. His breast is a little grayer, and the wing and tail linings are scarlet. Both flickers have large white spots on the back, above the tail, which show very plainly when they fly.

These two varieties of the flicker are found from the Atlantic to the Pacific. Their ways of living are the same, and what is said of one will do as well for the other.

A flicker hangs himself up to sleep. He takes a good hold of a tree trunk, or upright limb, with his grapnel-shaped toes, presses his stiff tail against the bark, and hangs there all night. When he flies, he goes in great waves, as if he were galloping through the air.

The nest of this woodpecker is a snug little room in a tree trunk, or sometimes a telegraph-pole. He usually selects a tree that is dead, or partly so, but sometimes he takes a solid one. The little room is cut out by the strong, sharp beaks of the pair. The door of this home is just a round hole rather high up on the trunk. A passage is cut straight in for a little way and then turns down, and there the room is made. It has to be of pretty good size, for the bird is fond of a large family. Five or six and occasionally more young flickers have been found in a nest.

Fashions change in the bird world as well as in the human. Woodpeckers more than any others are changing their habits, and improving their condition. They have found an easier way to get a home than to chisel it out of wood. Nowadays woodpeckers often cut a hole through a board which admits them into a garret, a church tower, or the walls of an unused building, and make the nest there. Thus they save themselves much labor. One even cut out a home in a haystack.

These birds have changed too, it is said, in their notions about eating. They do not think it necessary to dig out every mouthful from under tree bark. The flicker feeds on the ground. He eats many insects, but mostly ants. When insects are scarce, he eats many wild berries—dogwood, black alder, poke-berries, and others—and the seeds of weeds.

Young woodpeckers in the nest are fed mostly upon insects. When they get big enough to climb up to the door of their snug home, they stick their heads out and call for something to eat. Then one can hardly pass through the woods without hearing them, for they have good loud voices. And of course they are always hungry.

The way they are fed is by regurgitation. That is, the old bird swallows the food she gets, and when she wants to feed, she jerks it up again. She thrusts her bill far down the little one's throat, as I told you the hummingbird does. Then she gives three or four pokes as if she were hammering it down. A young flicker does not seem to know how to swallow. A lady once picked up a nestling who was hurt, and to get him to eat anything she had to poke it down his throat herself.

The gold-winged woodpecker is a lively bird, most interesting to know. He makes so many strange noises that I can't tell you half of them, and his ways are as queer as his notes. He does not sing much, but he is a great drummer. When he finds a tin roof, or eaves gutter that pleases him, he will drum on it till he drives the family nearly crazy. He seems particularly to delight in waking them all up in the morning.

He can sing, too. I have heard a flicker sing a droll little song, not very loud, swinging his body from side to side as he did it.

Another thing this bird can do is dance. Two flickers will stand opposite one another and take funny little steps, forward and back, and sideways. Then they will touch their bills together and go through several graceful figures. This has been seen several times by persons whose truthfulness can be relied upon.

The Red-headed Woodpecker is another common one of the family, especially in the Middle States. He is a little smaller than the flicker. No one can mistake this bird, he is so plainly marked. His whole head is bright red. The rest of him is black, or bluish black, with a large mass of white on the body and wings.

This woodpecker, too, has partly given up getting food from under the bark. He takes a good deal on the wing, like a flycatcher. Sometimes he goes to the ground for a large insect like a cricket or grasshopper, and he is fond of nuts, especially the little three-cornered beech-nut.

The red-head is beginning to store food for winter use, for most woodpeckers do not migrate. When beech-nuts are ripe, he gets great quantities of them, and packs them away in queer places, where he can find them when he wants them.

103

Some of his nuts the red-head puts in cavities in trees, others in knot-holes or under bark that is loose. Many he fits into cracks in the bark, and hammers in tight. He has been known to fill the cracks in a gate-post, and in railroad ties, and even to poke his nuts between the shingles on a roof. Any place where he can wedge a nut in he seems to think is a good one.

DOWNY WOODPECKER

A woodpecker can eat almost anything. Besides insects and nuts, he likes wild berries of all kinds—dogwood, cedar, and others that he finds in the woods.

The nest of the red-headed woodpecker is usually cut out in the dead top or limb of a tree. In prairie lands, where trees are scarce, he contents himself with telegraph-poles and fence-posts.

This bird is rather a dainty feeder. He does not swallow his food wherever he finds it, as many birds do. He likes a regular dining-table. So he takes it to some place on top of a fence-post or an old stump, where he has found or made a little hollow. There he puts his nut or acorn, picks it to pieces, and eats it in bits.

The young red-head is a good deal like his father, only his head is brown instead of red. A queer thing happened to a baby red-head in Indiana one summer. He was found on the ground, hopping about in a pitiful way, unable to fly. The parents and others of the woodpecker tribe were flying about him, much troubled, and trying to help him. But this young one had been hurt, or was not yet strong enough to get about. He acted as if he were half paralyzed, and he was wholly helpless. Once while the little bird was hobbling about and calling for something to eat, and no one was there to feed him, a robin happened to notice him. He took pity on the hungry baby, and brought him a nice worm, which he took very gladly.

But still more strange was the way the family cat acted toward the little stranger. When she saw him on the ground, she started for him. No doubt she meant to catch him, for she was a great bird hunter. When she got almost up to the little fellow, she seemed suddenly to notice that he was a baby, and helpless. At once her manner changed. She went up to him, and actually played with him in the gentlest way, not hurting him in the least. She did this several times before the bird got strong enough to fly. This is a true story.

The Californian Woodpecker takes the place of the red-head in California. He is most interesting because of one habit which gives him the common name of "carpenter woodpecker." This habit is of storing sweet acorns for winter use.

Other birds store acorns, but this bird has found out a new way. He drills a hole in the bark of a tree for each acorn by itself. It is generally a soft pine or cedar, and sometimes thousands of acorns are put in one tree. Often a trunk will be filled from near the ground up forty feet. The acorns are driven in point first, and so tightly that they have to be cut out with a knife. When a tree is filled, it is carefully guarded till they are needed.

Many people think they lay up these acorns for the worms that sometimes come into them. But Mr. John Muir, who lives right there, and knows them as well as anybody in the world, says the birds eat the sound acorns themselves. Sometimes, when food is scarce, Indians go to these trees and steal the poor birds' store. They have to chop the acorns out with hatchets. They often take a bushel from one tree.

These birds are more social than most woodpeckers. Often a party of them will be seen together. In his flight and his ways of eating this bird is like the red-headed woodpecker. Like him also, he is fond of clinging to a dead limb, and drumming, hours at a time.

But in looks the Californian and the red-headed woodpeckers are very different. The Western bird has only a cap of bright red. His back is glossy blue-black, and he has the same color on the breast. His other under parts are white, and he has a white patch on the wings, and another just above the tail.

The smallest of our woodpeckers is the Downy Woodpecker, who is not much bigger than an English sparrow. The picture shows two of these birds. In "The First Book of Birds" there is a picture of a flicker at his nest-hole.

FOOTNOTE:

_ See Appendix, 22.

XXX

THE KINGFISHER FAMILY

(*Alcedinidæ*)

Most of the Kingfisher family belong to the tropics, but we have one who is found all over the United States. This is the Belted Kingfisher.

BELTED KINGFISHER

The belted kingfisher is large and rather chunky. He is dark blue above and white below, with a bluish band across the breast. He has a fine crest and a big head, and he sits up straight as a hawk.

The tail of the kingfisher is short, and square at the end. His plumage is thick and oily, so that it does not hold wet. This is very important to him in the way he gets his food, for he is an expert fisherman. He lives alone, or with his mate, near the water,—a lake, or pond, or small stream.

This bird's way of getting fish is to dive for them. You may have seen him splash into the water out of sight, and in a moment come up with a small fish in his beak. Then he goes back to his perch and beats the fish to death, before he swallows it. He swallows it whole and head first, because the fins might stick in his throat if he took it tail first. After a while he throws up a little ball of the bones, scales, and skin of the fish he has eaten. It is said that the kingfisher can take a very large fish. One was shot who had swallowed a fish so long that the tail stuck out of his mouth, and could not get down.

The nest of the kingfisher is in the bank of a river or lake. The birds first cut a passage or hallway. Sometimes this is only four feet long, and straight. But when stones or roots are in the way, it will be much longer and have many turns. At the end of this passage is the kingfisher nursery. This is a round room nearly a foot across, with a roof rounded up over it. It is a little higher than the passageway so that water will not run into it.

Sometimes it takes the birds two or three weeks to make one of these nests, as we might expect when we think they have only beaks and feet to work with. Usually it does not take so long. If the pair are not disturbed, they will use the same nest year after year. Sometimes the bed for the nestlings is of dry grass. One was found in which the bed was entirely of the bones and scales of fish.

Mr. Baily has told us about a family of kingfisher little folk whom he studied and photographed. He dug down to the nest from above, and was careful not to hurt them and to put them back safely. First Mr. Baily took a picture of them when two days old. They were queer-

106

looking objects, with eyes not open, and not a feather to their backs. They were not so young but that they had one notion in their little round heads. That was to cuddle up close together. They were not used to much room in their dark cradle.

When Mr. Baily laid them out on the ground, they at once crawled up together and made themselves into a sort of ball. They put their bare wings and their bills over one another, and held on so that one could not be moved without the others. After they had sat for their picture they were carefully put back, and the nest was covered up again.

When the nestlings were nine days old, the nest was opened again, and another picture taken. The little ones had grown a good deal in these few days. Their eyes were open, and they were fast getting their feather coats on. But they were just as fond of being close together as before.

After this the birds were left in their home till they were twenty-three days old, and it seemed about time for them to come out. When the nest was opened this time, it was found that the family had moved. The old room was filled up with earth, and a new one made farther up. No doubt the old birds thought the man too curious about their babies. The young birds were ready to fly, and two of them did take to their wings when they came to daylight.

There is a very old fable about the kingfisher, who was called the halcyon. It is told in the first book that was ever written about birds (so far as I know). The author was Aristotle, a Greek who lived three hundred years before Christ. The story is, that the bird builds a nest that floats on the sea, and for seven days before and seven days after the shortest winter day, the sea stays calm, so that the nest may not be hurt. During the first seven days she builds her nest, and in the second seven she hatches out the young. These fourteen days were called halcyon days. You may find more about this curious story in the encyclopædias.

FOOTNOTE:

See Appendix, 23.

XXXI

THE CUCKOO FAMILY

(*Cuculidæ*)

Most of the cuckoo family live in a hotter climate than ours, but we have a few of them. They are beautiful birds, with some peculiar ways.

YELLOW-BILLED CUCKOO

Cuckoos are rather slim in form, with very long tails, and bills a little curved. Their toes are divided like woodpeckers' toes, two turned forward and two back. In the Eastern States we have but two, the yellow-billed and the black-billed. Best known in the East is the Yellow-billed Cuckoo, and in California the Western Yellow-billed, or California, Cuckoo.

This bird has several names. In some places he is called the rain crow, and in other places the wood pigeon; but of course he is neither a crow nor a pigeon. He is a graceful bird, with plumage like satin. He is a soft brown above and white below, but he is so shy that he is not so often seen as heard. His call or song is a loud, yet not harsh "kuk-kuk-kuk" many times repeated. Sometimes it begins slow and grows faster till the notes run into each other, and then grows slow again, ending in a sort of "cow-cow-cow;" but it does not always do so.

The cuckoo does not manage her nursery affairs as other birds do. Most birds lay an egg a day, or every other day, so that they hatch about the same time; but this bird doesn't mind if several days come between. Thus it happens that one or more little cuckoos hatch out before the rest are ready, and it is common to find little ones of several ages in the same nest. There may be one nearly grown, another just beginning to get feathers, and a third one not yet out of the egg.

There is another droll thing that may be found in a cuckoo's nest. When the feathers begin to grow out on young birds, they come wrapped in little sheaths. In most cases these sheaths burst open and the feathers show, when they are a little way out. But in this family it is different. The sheath does not open, says Mr. Dugmore, till the feathers have grown their full length. Till that happens, the youngster looks as if he were stuck all over with white pins on his black body.

You have heard, or read, that the cuckoo lays eggs in other birds' nests, and leaves her young to be brought up by others. Do not forget that the bird who does that is the European cuckoo—not ours. Our cuckoos build nests, though very poor ones, sometimes hardly more than a platform of sticks.

This bird is useful to us, for he eats some of our most troublesome insects,—such as tent caterpillars, which few birds like to eat because they are so hairy, and other insects with spines that are poisonous, and so generally avoided.

The cuckoo is graceful in flight. He goes swiftly, without noise, and seems to glide through the thickest foliage with ease.

I once found a young bird tumbling about on the ground. He was trying to fly, but was not able to go much more than a foot at a time. He was giving strange calls, which were answered from the woods beside the road by a low tapping sound. I thought of course the little one was a woodpecker and his mother was doing the knocking. It was so dark I could not see him well. After some trouble I caught him and was going to take a good look at him to see who he was before I let him go. As I grasped him he gave a shriek, and out from the thick trees popped a cuckoo. She alighted on a low branch outside and gave such a cry of distress that I knew at once it was her baby I held in my hand.

I suppose the poor mother thought I wanted to carry the youngster off. I couldn't bear to have a bird think that for a minute; so I opened my hands and away he went, half flying, half scrambling up the road, while the mother slipped back into the woods. In a moment she began again her hollow-sounding calls, which I had thought were woodpecker tappings.

FOOTNOTE:

 See Appendix, 24.

XXXII

THE OWL FAMILY

(Bubonidæ)

Owls differ from all other birds in having eyes that look forward like ours. They have also a broad face, which is made to look even wider by the feathers which stand out around the eyes.

Owls cannot turn their eyes in the sockets, so they have to turn the whole head to see to one side. Many of them have tufts of feathers like horns, which they can stand up or lay down as they choose. These are called horned owls. An owl's legs are covered with feathers, sometimes down to the toes. The whole plumage of this bird is soft and fluffy, so that he can fly without making any noise. This is important to him, for he lives mostly on mice, and he never could catch one if he made much noise getting about.

The owl's mate looks like him, and—what is unusual among birds—she is larger than he. Because they come out in the evening, when we cannot see them well, we know very little of their ways. They are more often heard than seen. Their voices are generally mournful, but that is no reason why they should be feared.

All birds have control over some of their feathers, that is, they can make them stand up or lie down as they choose. But owls have more than any other bird. An owl can alter his shape or size so that he will look like another bird.

Mr. Bolles says that a large owl can change from a mass of bristling feathers a yard wide, to a slim, sleek brown post only a few inches wide. When he does this, one cannot see him, though he may be in plain sight. His colors blend with a tree trunk, or stump, and he can stand without stirring for an hour, and likes to do it.

Mr. Bolles had owls in the house, and watched them closely. He has told us some curious things about their ways. He says that when one steps daintily across the floor, his feathers tuck themselves up as a lady holds up her gown.

This moving of the feathers sometimes looks very droll. When eating, the feathers around the mouth, which might get soiled, draw back out of the way. And when an owl wants to hide his food, he stands over it, and the feathers droop down like a curtain to screen it from view. When Mrs. Bolles wanted to sketch an owl, he kept changing his shape all the time, though he did not seem to move at all.

Another man who had a pet owl says that the bird would stand before him and throw back his breast feathers each side, just as a man throws open his coat.

The owlets come out of the egg dressed in soft, fluffy down. In some of the family it is gray, in others it is snowy white. They are carefully fed and reared by their loving parents.

A funny story is told by a man who wanted to see what was in an owl's nest. He lifted the mother bird out, and to his surprise the whole family came out with her. She held on to one little one, and each one held on to the next, and so he had the whole owl family in a cluster, like a bunch of grapes.

The Screech Owl is the best known of this family. He is found, under slightly different forms, all over our country. In Florida he is smaller and darker than in the Middle States. In California he is larger and grayer, and in the Rocky Mountains somewhat lighter. But he acts in about the same way, wherever he lives.

In the East the screech owl is found in two colors. Some have reddish feathers, others have gray. The wise men have not yet found any reason for this difference.

The screech owl is badly named, for his song is not a screech. It is a sort of trembling sound, and in some places he is called the "shivering owl," which is a much better name for him than screech owl. If one does not know who makes it, it is rather a weird song in the dark; but if one knows the pretty gray bird, it is sweet and pleasing.

The bird comes out before it is quite pitch dark. He may often be seen against the sky, standing on a branch, bowing and swaying back and forth, while he utters strange notes of many kinds. He has plenty to say for himself. But you must keep as still as a mouse if you want to see him. If he can see to catch a mouse in the dark, you may be sure he can see you.

Generally the screech owl makes a nest in a hollow tree or a deserted woodpecker nest, and comes out only at night. What he likes best to eat is mice, and mice too come out at night. The way he eats is curious, as I told you in "The First Book of Birds."

A few years ago a screech owl went through a broken window into the attic of a house in New Jersey, and lived there all winter. The family were bird-lovers, so they let her stay. She liked it so well that the next spring she made her nest there and hatched out three little owls. The little ones were not at all afraid of people, and a son of the family made many photographs of them.

After the owlets were grown, the whole family disappeared, and lived out of doors the rest of the summer. But when cold weather came, the old birds came back and stayed all winter again. They have made their home in that attic, and reared a brood every spring since. They are always very social among themselves. They talk and sing, and make many sorts of noises.

One of the queerest of the owl family is the little Burrowing Owl of the West. The Florida Burrowing Owl, found in Florida, differs only a little from the Western bird. The burrowing owl is a comical-looking fellow, only about as large as a robin. He has very long legs for an owl, and is dressed in grayish brown.

This bird is said to have very polite manners. In some places he is called the "how-do-you-do owl." He is always bowing, and turning from side to side, and seems to be greeting you as you come near him.

The burrowing owl likes a comfortable home underground, out of the way of enemies. In the West, where he lives, prairie dogs are plentiful, and they are always digging out passages and rooms, more than they can use. So the owl has no trouble in finding empty quarters to live in.

But in California, and places where are none of the digging dogs, the little owl rooms with some of the ground squirrels that burrow there. He must have an underground home in that land where trees are scarce, and he has no fancy for digging. Even if he wanted to dig, his feet are not fitted for it like the feet of the little beasts.

The burrowing owl has no trouble in taking a house where he finds one to suit him, for he's a savage little fellow. He can kill squirrels and prairie dogs much bigger than himself, and even rattlesnakes, which take lodgings in the prairie dog houses also. He feeds upon all these creatures. He eats also crickets, scorpions, and many troublesome insects. This makes him valuable to farmers, for nearly all these creatures destroy his crops.

Remember, too, that birds have great appetites; as I have told you, they eat more than their own weight every day. In that way they dispose of enormous numbers of pests. It almost seems as if a bird were a sort of eating machine, made on purpose to work for us. We should never forget this.

This bird, like most others, makes many different sounds. His song is a soft "coo-oo," something like that of a mourning dove. When a stranger comes to his home and he is there, he gives a rattle which sounds like a rattlesnake. This scares people, and perhaps animals, away, for no one wants to meet a rattlesnake in a dark hole. I wonder if the bird learned this trick living in the same house with the snake.

The Department of Agriculture has proved owls to be among the most useful of birds. Their food is almost entirely of hurtful creatures, and they come out at night when other birds are asleep and are ready to hunt the pests which do the same.

FOOTNOTE:

_ See Appendix, 25.

XXXIII

THE BARN OWL FAMILY

(*Strigidæ*)

This is a small family of which we have but one member in America, the American Barn Owl. He is found all over the country, as far north as southern New England, but he is one of the shyest of birds. He comes out only at night, and hides so well in the day that he is not often seen, even where he is common. So very little is known of his ways.

When he does happen to come out, and any one sees him, a great deal is said about him. For he is a very odd-looking fellow indeed. He is all in gray and white, clouded and speckled and barred, and his face is the strangest of bird faces. It is three-cornered, and looks more like a monkey's than a bird's. If he shows this face in the daylight, he is generally caught or shot, and the newspapers make a great fuss about him. Some one says he looks like a toothless little old woman, with a hooked nose.

Happily for the barn owl, he does not often come out. He loves quiet more than anything. He seeks a hidden, safe place, not only for a nest, but to spend his days in. He is almost the only bird who may be said to live in a home.

When house hunting, this bird will take a snug cavity in a tree, or an empty building. He does not despise an old mining shaft, or a burrow in the ground. He delights in a church steeple or a barn. Almost any place that is quiet and out of sight of the world will suit him.

All day the barn owl stays at home. But in the evening he comes out for his dinner, and then there is havoc among the small animals. Rats, ground squirrels, mice, bats, small snakes, grasshoppers, and almost anything else that is eatable are welcome to him. He should be protected because he is so useful.

This bird is an amiable fellow too. He has been known to live pleasantly in a church tower with pigeons, whom he could easily kill to eat if he wished. He is a hearty eater himself, besides feeding a family of five or six little fuzzy white owlets great quantities of food.

One of these owls has lived for years in a tower of the Smithsonian Institution in Washington. In the Zoölogical Collection of that city, there was, not long ago, another of the family alive. Wishing to have more of them in the Zoo, some one watched the nest of the tower bird. When her little family of seven was about ready to fly, he took them away, and gave them to their caged relative. She promptly adopted the whole party, and reared them with the greatest care. No doubt she was glad to have something to do. Life in a cage must be very tiresome for wild birds and beasts.

Mr. Reed of Philadelphia has told us how a pet barn owl threw up the castings. These, you know, are the bones and skin of mice and other creatures which are thrown up awhile after eating. He would bow his head and shake it very hard. Then raise it and jerk out the little ball.

This bird was very tame. The place where he liked best to sit was on the arm or shoulder of his master. If the man wanted to do anything except play with him, he had to get a stuffed bird to amuse the living one. It was like a doll for a baby girl. When the owl was not perfectly comfortable, he kept up a constant cry, so his master had to keep him well entertained and fed.

The note of the barn owl is a wild screech. One is sometimes heard making this sound, but he is never heard flying, for, like other owls, he is dressed in soft feathers that make no rustle.

FOOTNOTE:

_ See Appendix, 26.

XXXIV

THE HAWK AND EAGLE FAMILY

(*Falconidæ*)

This is a family of birds of prey. That is, birds who live entirely on living animals, which they hunt and catch for themselves. Owls are also birds of prey, but they do their hunting by night, while this family work by day.

SPARROW HAWK

Like all birds, hawks are well fitted for what they have to do. They have long wings, so that they can fly swiftly and long at a time, to follow up the prey. They have sharp, curved claws, made for grasping and holding things. Their hooked beak is the best kind for cutting and tearing meat.

Most of these birds work for us the whole time, as do the owls. For they eat the same destructive animals, and they eat an enormous number. Yet we have a foolish prejudice against them, because two or three of them sometimes take poultry and game birds. Even when these birds do take our poultry and game birds, some good is done. For they naturally catch the weak ones who are not able to get out of their way. And it is better for the whole race of these birds that the weak ones should not live. It leaves the rest stronger, and better able to make their way in the world.

This family is found all over the world. It includes birds of all sizes, from one as small as a sparrow to one who spreads his wings ten feet. In our country we have neither the smallest nor the largest. Of those you are likely to see, the least is the American Sparrow Hawk, who is not much larger than a robin, and the greatest is the Bald Eagle, who is sometimes a yard from the tip of his beak to the end of his tail.

Hawks have wonderful eyes like a telescope and microscope in one, as I have told you in "The First Book of Birds." In eating without knife and fork, they often swallow food whole and throw up castings like the owls.

In catching their prey these birds use their feet instead of their beaks. Even those who hunt grasshoppers and crickets seize them in their claws. Their feet are quite as useful as hands. In them they carry material for the nest as well as food for the little ones. The claws are powerful weapons of war, too. A hawk who is ready to fight throws himself on his back and presents his claws to the enemy. Few people would like to be grappled by those terrible claws.

Hawks and eagles have wonderful wing power. Some of them can stay far up in the air an hour at a time. They go up in great circles with wings held stiffly out and not beating, till out of sight. Men have not yet been able to see quite how it is done. It is probably by using the wings as sailors use their sails, and making the wind carry them.

113

The one of this family I shall tell you about is the Fish Hawk, or American Osprey, because he is found all over the United States. He is one of those which you will be most likely to see, and want to know about.

The osprey is a large bird, about two feet long. He is dressed in chocolate brown, with white breast and white tips to many of his feathers. His head feathers are long, and lie back on his neck, giving a peculiar shape to the head, by which you may know him at once. These feathers too are white, so that as he flies over he looks as if he were bald. He has feet marvelously fitted to hold slippery fish. The talons are sharp, and the toes long, and rough on the under side, so that nothing can get away from them.

The fish hawk is a social bird and fond of his home. Though he migrates, he comes back to the old place, year after year. He likes the top of a stout tree to build in. It needs to be stout, for he makes a very big nest, and adds to it every season. It generally kills the tree, if it is not dead when he begins. If there are no trees to be had, or if there are too many birds for the trees at hand, some of them will nest on the ground, for they like to keep near their friends. The nest is made of sticks and all the rubbish the birds can collect. Such things are found as an old broom, a boy's sail-boat, a rag doll, and others as absurd.

The young fish hawk is a pretty little fellow in white down. He is three or four weeks in the egg, and a long time in the nest, and is helpless a good deal longer. He is fed on fish like his parents. For this bird deserves his name; he is a fisherman, and always takes his food from the water. Fortunately he usually selects the poorer kinds of fish, which men do not care to eat, and so he is not called an enemy by the fishermen.

But the hard-working osprey has an enemy, who makes it his business to rob him. The way the fish hawk gets his food is to dive for it. He hovers over the water till he sees a fish near the surface that suits him. Then he closes his wings and dives like a shot. He plunges in often over his head, and seizes the fish in his claws or talons. Then he rises, and shaking off the water flies toward his family, with their dinner.

AMERICAN OSPREY OR FISH HAWK

But then appears the robber, the bald eagle, I'm sorry to say, who prefers stealing his food to hunting for himself. He rushes furiously at the fish hawk, who is obliged to drop his load to defend himself. Then the eagle seizes it, often before it reaches the ground, and flies off, while the osprey goes back to his fishing.

But the osprey is learning something, like the rest of the birds. On the shore of New Jersey there is a place where men fish with great nets, and bring in hundreds of fish every day. The birds have noted how much better men are at their trade of fishing than they are. So they have thought out an easier way to get food than to dive for it. Perhaps they got the hint from the eagle.

Wherever the fish hawks got the idea, it is now the common custom for them to sit on the poles that hold the net and wait. When it is drawn up filled with flopping fish, each bird dives down and secures one for himself. And he takes time to choose, too. If there is one of a kind he particularly likes, he goes for that one.

Fish hawks, like other birds, are very fond of their little ones. A gentleman who had been traveling in the West told me this little story. He, with a party who were wandering over a wild part of the country, accidentally set fire to a bit of woods on the shore of Lake Superior. On one of the trees was a fish hawk's nest with young birds. As soon as the smoke began to spread, the old birds grew uneasy, and circled about their tree, going often to the nest.

The men who had done the mischief, and who had then taken to their boat, were noting the spread of the fire. They watched the birds to see what they would do. When the fire at last reached their tree, the loving parents turned with one accord, plunged down into the nest, and all perished together. They could easily have saved themselves, but they could not desert their nestlings.

FOOTNOTE:

See Appendix, 27.

XXXV

THE SCAVENGER FAMILY

(*Cathartidæ*)

This is one of the most useful of bird families. But it is not very pleasant to meet, for the work it has to do makes it rather repulsive to us.

The vultures are scavengers. They dispose of vast quantities of carrion and other offensive matter. In doing this they make it possible for people to live in places where they could not live without the service of these birds.

The common vulture in the United States is the Turkey Vulture, or Turkey Buzzard. He is a large bird, with head and neck bare of feathers. In shape and size he is a good deal like a turkey. He is a familiar bird all over the country, except in New England and other northern parts, and is usually seen soaring about in the air, looking for food. Beautiful and graceful he looks away up against the sky. He sails around as if he weighed nothing, with wing feathers spread at the tip like fingers. But he is not so pretty when he comes to the ground, for he is very clumsy and awkward in getting about.

The turkey buzzard nests almost anywhere; he is not at all particular—on the ground, in a hollow stump, or tree. The young are comfortably dressed in white down, but they are not pretty. They are as awkward as their parents, and have a way of hanging their heads as if they were ashamed of themselves. That is not the reason, however; their work is something we could not do without. It is because they are too weak to hold themselves up.

I once saw a funny sight. A party of eighteen or twenty great buzzards had come to the ground to get their dinner. They were all very busily engaged just the other side of a fence, so that I could not see them at their feast.

Suddenly a mockingbird that I was watching flew over and alighted on the fence. He stood there a minute, looking sharply down at them, and flirting his tail in a saucy way. All at once, to my great surprise, he gave a loud cry and flung himself down right among the great birds.

I was frightened. I thought one peck from one of their strong beaks would kill the little fellow. But instead of that, the whole party of buzzards flew up in a panic, as if they were afraid of him. Then the mockingbird, who looked like a midget beside them, hopped back upon the fence, and burst into a loud song of victory. He knew the turkey buzzard better than I did. No one likes to get very near this bird, so very little is known about his ways.

FOOTNOTE:

See Appendix, 28.

APPENDIX

CHARACTERS OF THE NORTH AMERICAN REPRESENTATIVES OF THE FAMILIES MENTIONED IN THIS BOOK

Note.—These characters, though correct, are untechnically given, and are such as may be observed on the "bird in the bush" while the added hints on habits, etc., will be found helpful in identification.

1. Turdidæ: Thrushes.

Medium size; bill shorter than head, straight or nearly so; bristles (hair-like feathers) at corner of mouth; wings rather pointed, and longer than tail; tail-feathers wider towards the end, the whole somewhat fan-shaped. Young in first feathers speckled and streaked, very different from the adults. Sexes nearly alike (except robin, varied thrush, and bluebird). (Ridgway.)

Food: insects, earthworms, and sometimes fruit.

These birds are all singers and build rude nests. Found usually on the lower part of trees in the woods (except robin and bluebird) or on the ground, where they get most of their food.

2. Sylviidæ: Kinglets and Gnatcatchers.

This family is divided into two subfamilies.

Kinglets: Very small; bill slender, much shorter than head, straight to near tip, then slightly curved; bristles at corner of mouth; wings longer than tail; tail slightly forked, feathers pointed; legs long; claws much curved. Young without markings on head. (Ridgway.)

Food: insects.

Very small, active, musical birds, usually found flitting about in trees.

Gnatcatchers: Very small and slim; bill slender and short, nearly as long as head, notched at tip; bristles at corner of mouth; wings shorter than tail and rounded; tail long and moderately graduated, feathers rounded; legs rather long; toes small. (Ridgway.)

Active, beautiful nest builders, found in the tops of trees. Insectivorous.

3. Paridæ: Nuthatches, Titmice, etc.

This family is divided into three subfamilies.

Nuthatches: Smaller than English sparrow; bill sharp, pointed, higher than wide, about as long as head; bristles over nostrils; wings pointed; tail very short, nearly even, feathers soft; legs stout. (Ridgway.)

Parents nearly alike; food, insects.

Found on the trunks and large limbs of trees.

Titmice: Usually smaller than English sparrow; bill stout, conical, shorter than head; nasal feathers turned forward; tail longer than wing. (Ridgway.)

Food: insects. Parents alike, and young the same. No noticeable change of plumage with season.

Wren-Tits and Bush-Tits: Very small; bill short and conical; tail rounded. Sexes alike.

4. Certhiidæ: Creepers.

Smaller than English sparrow; bill slender and curved downward; wings rather pointed, long as tail; tail graduated, stiff, with long, sharp-pointed feathers; claws long and strongly curved. (Ridgway.)

Food: insects. Sexes alike, and young the same. Found circling tree trunks.

5. Troglodytidæ: Wrens and Mocking Thrushes.

This family is divided into two subfamilies.

Wrens: Smaller than English sparrow; bill slender, sometimes long and arched; no bristles at corner of mouth; wings rounded; tail usually held up. (Ridgway.)

Parents and young alike. Food: insects. Singers. Found near the ground.

Mocking Thrushes: Larger than English sparrow; bill slender, mostly rather long; bristles at corner of mouth; wings rounded; tail longer than wings; appear like thrushes; fine singers. (Ridgway.)

Sexes nearly alike. Food, insects and fruit. Some of them found in bushy borders of woods, some about gardens and houses, and others in various places.

6. Cinclidæ: Dippers.

Larger than English sparrow; bill slender, shorter than head; wings short, stiff and rounded; tail shorter than wings, soft and square; claws strongly curved; plumage soft and compact; body stout, thickset. Sexes alike. (Coues.)

Food: water insects and larvæ. Found in and about the brooks of the Rocky Mountains and other mountains of the West.

7. Motacillidæ: Wagtails and Pipits.

Larger than English sparrow; bill slender, cone shaped, nearly as high as wide, at base; short bristles at corner of mouth; wings rather long and pointed; tail narrow and slightly forked; legs rather long; hind claw very long, sharp and slightly curved. (Ridgway.)

Sexes alike. Food: insects. Found on the ground, where they walk, and wag their tails.

8. Mniotiltidæ: Warblers.

It is almost impossible to characterize this family, there are so many varieties. With few exceptions they are very small and beautifully colored birds, sexes unlike, and changes of plumage with age and season. Some are found in the tops of trees, some on bushes, and some on the ground. Food: insects. (Coues.)

9. Vireonidæ: Vireos.

Generally smaller than an English sparrow, and more slender; bill notched in both mandibles; tail rather short, nearly even, of narrow feathers; front toes more or less united. (Ridgway.)

Food: insects. Constant singers. Sexes alike and young the same, without spots or streaks. Some found in trees in the woods, and others about towns where English sparrows are not too numerous.

10. Laniidæ: Shrikes.

Larger than an English sparrow; bill powerful, tip hooked and notched; wings short, rounded; tail long and much graduated. (Ridgway.)

Food: insects, small mammals, and sometimes birds. Sexes alike, and young the same. Found on outside of low trees, fences, telegraph wires, and peaks of roofs.

11. Ampelidæ: Waxwings, etc.

Somewhat larger than an English sparrow; bill short, broad and rather flat; head with pointed crest; wings long and pointed; tail short, narrow, even; legs of moderate length. (Ridgway.)

Food: insects and fruit. Sexes usually alike. Found in trees in woods and in shade and orchard trees.

12. Hirundinidæ: Swallows.

About the size of an English, sparrow; bill short, flat, and very broad at the head; mouth opens back nearly to the eyes; wings long and scythe shaped; tail forked; legs short; feet weak; plumage compact and usually lustrous. (Ridgway.)

Food: insects. Sexes usually alike, and young a little different. Found in flocks, in the air, on roofs or fences or telegraph wires, sometimes on trees.

13. Tanagridæ: Tanagers.

Larger than an English sparrow; bill conical, notched, bristles; wings longer than tail; tail of moderate length, somewhat notched; legs rather short. (Ridgway.)

Food: insects. Sexes unlike. Found on trees in the woods.

14. Fringillidæ: Finches.

Mostly about the size of an English sparrow, some smaller, some larger; bill short, high, and strong, turned down at the back corner; wings and tail variable. (Ridgway.)

Seed and insect eaters. Found everywhere—on trees, bushes, on ground, in woods, fields, and about houses.

15. Icteridæ: Blackbirds, Orioles, etc.

Larger than an English sparrow; bill straight or gently curved; mouth turned down at corners; tail rather long and rounded; legs rather short. Includes birds of very different habits. (Ridgway.)

Food: seeds and insects. Sexes generally unlike. Found everywhere, on trees, in marshes, in woods. Many gregarious, found in flocks, some except in nesting season, and others all the year round.

16. Corvidæ: Crows and Jays.
Larger than a robin. There are two subfamilies.
Crows: Bill longer than head; wings long and pointed; tail rather short and even.
Jays: Bill shorter than head; wings short and rounded. (Ridgway.)
Food: almost everything—seeds, fruit, sometimes eggs and young birds. Found in woody places.

17. Alaudidæ: Larks.
Larger than an English sparrow; bill short, conical, frontal feathers extend along the side; wings pointed; claw on hind toe very long and nearly straight. (Ridgway.)
Food: insects. Sexes nearly alike. Found on ground in fields and roads.

18. Tyrannidæ: Flycatchers.
Mostly larger than an English sparrow; bill broad, flattened, curved downward at end, and notched at tip; bristles along the gape; wings and tail variable. (Ridgway.)
Entirely insectivorous. Found in woods and fields and about houses.

19. Trochilidæ: Hummingbirds.
Our smallest birds; bill slender, sharp, and straight, usually longer than head; wings long and pointed; legs short; feet small and weak; claws curved and sharp. (Ridgway.)
Food: tiny insects and the honey of flowers. Sexes unlike. Found about flowers.

20. Micropodidæ: Swifts.
About the size of an English sparrow; bill very small, triangular, much broader than high, without bristles; wings long and pointed; legs short; feet weak; tail very short, ending in stiff spines; plumage compact. (Ridgway.)
Food: entirely insects. Sexes alike. Found in the air or inside chimneys or hollow trees.

21. Caprimulgidæ: Goatsuckers.
Larger than a robin; bill very short; gape enormously long and wide; mouth open to behind the eyes; wings long; plumage soft. (Ridgway.)
Food: insects. Sexes nearly alike. One species found in the edge of woods, and another species about towns.

22. Picidæ: Woodpeckers.
Larger than an English sparrow; bill usually straight, pointed or chisel-shaped at tip; tongue extensile and except in one species barbed at point; tail stiff and feathers pointed at tip for a prop; toes, except in three-toed species, two forward and two backward for climbing. (Ridgway.)
Insectivorous. Sexes unlike. Found on trees (except one species) in woods or orchards.

23. Alcedinidæ: Kingfishers.
Usually larger than a robin; bill long and straight; tongue small; head large, crested; wings short; legs small; outer and middle toe united half their length. (Ridgway.)
Food: fishes. Sexes slightly unlike. Found by water.

24. Cuculidæ: Cuckoos.
Larger than a robin; bill narrow and high, rather long and curved downward; wings long; tail long, soft, and rounded; toes in pairs. (Ridgway.)

Insectivorous. Sexes alike. Found on trees.

25. Bubonidæ: Owls.

Mostly larger than a robin, a few smaller; bill hooked; eyes directed forward and surrounded by radiating feathers; plumage soft and lax; feathers beside forehead often stand up like ear tufts; legs usually feathered; feet sometimes feathered. (Ridgway.)

Sexes alike. Flesh eaters. Usually nocturnal. Most species found in holes in trees or old buildings.

26. Strigidæ: Barn Owls.

Much larger than a robin; bill hooked; eyes very small; triangular-shaped eye disk; tail emarginate; claws sharp and strong; very downy plumage. (Ridgway).

Food: mice and other small mammals. Sexes alike. Exclusively nocturnal. Found in barns and deserted buildings.

27. Falconidæ: Hawks and Eagles.

(There are several subfamilies.)

Mostly very large birds; bill strongly hooked; eyes directed sideways; eyelids with lashes; toes never feathered. (Ridgway.)

Carnivorous and insectivorous. Sexes usually alike, but female larger.

28. Cathartidæ: American Vultures.

Large as a turkey, one species much larger; whole head and sometimes neck bare of feathers; eyes prominent; tail rounded. (Ridgway.)

Food: carrion. Found sailing about in the air.